HARD LESSONS FROM
THE HURT BUSINESS

HARD LESSONS
from the
HURT BUSINESS

BOXING AND THE

ART OF LIFE

Ed Latimore

PORTFOLIO | PENGUIN

Portfolio / Penguin
An imprint of Penguin Random House LLC
1745 Broadway, New York, NY 10019
penguinrandomhouse.com

Most Portfolio books are available at a discount when purchased in quantity for sales
promotions or corporate use. Special editions, which include personalized covers, excerpts,
and corporate imprints, can be created when purchased in large quantities. For more
information, please call (212) 572-2232 or e-mail specialmarkets@penguinrandomhouse.com.
Your local bookstore can also assist with discounted bulk purchases using the Penguin
Random House corporate Business-to-Business program. For assistance in locating
a participating retailer, e-mail B2B@penguinrandomhouse.com.

BOOK DESIGN BY MEIGHAN CAVANAUGH

Library of Congress Cataloging-in-Publication Data

Names: Latimore, Ed, 1985– author
Title: Hard lessons from the hurt business : boxing and the art of life / Ed Latimore.
Other titles: Boxing and the art of life
Description: [New York, New York] : Portfolio, [2025]
Identifiers: LCCN 2024044895 (print) | LCCN 2024044896 (ebook) |
ISBN 9780593716366 hardcover | ISBN 9780593716373 ebook
Subjects: LCSH: Latimore, Ed, 1985– |
African American boxers—Pennsylvania—Pittsburgh—Biography |
Boxers (Sports)—Pennsylvania—Pittsburgh—Biography |
Pittsburgh (Pa.)—Biography | Self-actualization (Psychology)
Classification: LCC GV1132.L348 A3 2025 (print) |
LCC GV1132.L348 (ebook) | DDC 796.83092 [B]—dc23/eng/20250509
LC record available at https://lccn.loc.gov/2024044895
LC ebook record available at https://lccn.loc.gov/2024044896

Printed in the United States of America
1st Printing

The authorized representative in the EU for product safety and compliance
is Penguin Random House Ireland, Morrison Chambers, 32 Nassau Street,
Dublin D02 YH68, Ireland, https://eu-contact.penguin.ie.

To my son Henry,

simultaneously the greatest motivation for

and distraction from writing this book.

I took the hard way through life

so that you won't have to.

CONTENTS

AUTHOR'S NOTE

When kids call me up, I say, "Let me ask you an honest question: Have your parents ever hit you?" If they say no, I say, "I don't think you belong in boxing."

–Hal Adonis, president of USA Boxing from 2009 to 2012

To become a skilled fighter, you need more than just physical strength. You need a certain kind of spirit—a spirit forged in the crucible of life's harshest trials. You only become that person when you've endured life's blows and sought healing from them. Grit and resilience aren't just inborn traits; they're the products of adversity. Whether you're up against oppressive parents, relentless bullies, or the unforgiving grind of life itself, you learn to fight by fighting.

This principle isn't confined to the ring. It's a universal truth that extends to every field where greatness is pursued. Great artists, business moguls, and athletes alike are often driven by deep-seated self-doubts, born from early failures and mistreatment. Their craft becomes their battleground—a way to outrun the shadows of their past and strive for a brighter future.

In my own journey, boxing emerged as my chosen form of therapy. But to understand why I turned to the sport, you need to grasp the depth of the pain and struggle that led me there. This is more than just a story about punching and bruising—it's about how fighting became my path to healing, strength, and self-discovery.

As you delve into my story, you'll find not just a chronicle of battles fought and won but a tool kit for overcoming your own adversities. You'll see how I transformed life's brutal lessons into a blueprint for resilience, and how you can do the same. This book is about finding your fight, embracing it, and emerging stronger on the other side.

HARD LESSONS FROM
THE HURT BUSINESS

I

A Hard Childhood Makes It Easy to Accept Harsh Truths

was born in 1985 in Pittsburgh, Pennsylvania, and spent the first ten years of my life in the Terrace Village housing projects in the Hill District. This was the height of the crack epidemic, and while the entire nation was dealing with the devastating effects of this new drug, poor Black Americans were getting hit the hardest.

Now, I don't want to give the impression that the projects were a nice place to live before crack. You didn't move to the projects because you couldn't decide between a ranch-style home in the suburbs and a downtown condominium. Chris Rock said it best in his comedy special *Bring the Pain*: "Crack is destroying the ghetto? Yeah, like the ghetto was so nice before crack!"

Even before crack came to the ghetto, the ghetto was where

you went when you had nowhere else to go. Crack fed the fire of violence and crime and then fanned those flames to incinerate anything in the ghetto that resembled peaceful life in a developed nation. Gunshots, gang violence, and hard drugs were the backdrop of my everyday life from as early as I can remember.

When I was four, my babysitter left out what I thought was a toy water gun. I decided to have some fun and spray it around a bit. Well, it turns out that the "water gun" was a syringe, and the "water" it was filled with was heroin.

One thing I've always admired about hard-drug users is their unapologetic attitude toward their addiction. Years later, my mom told me that the woman who left out the needle showed no shame—she just wanted her money back.

"I need some money for this, Miss Faye. That baggie of horse was twenty!"

For my mom's part, it wasn't the woman's addiction that bothered her; it was the careless placement of drugs around a child. My mom wasn't indifferent to having a drug user babysit, she just chose the lesser evil: leave me home alone or let the neighborhood junkie watch me.

I've always made a lot of jokes about drugs and the ghetto. Seventeenth-century French playwright Jean Racine once wrote, "Life is a comedy to those who think and a tragedy to those who feel." My sense of humor is how I cope with the residual trauma from my childhood. I figure I can either laugh a little or cry a lot. I choose to laugh.

After the argument about the wasted heroin, my mom had to find a new babysitter. Choosing not to work, and instead relying on welfare, food stamps, and child support was always an option, but it was easily the worst one. Food stamps can only be used for food, and hardly enough of it to support a family. The only reason I got three meals a day was because I relied on free lunches during the school year and community meal programs during the summer. This was in addition to our biweekly trips to the food bank.

We lived in subsidized public housing projects. We didn't have to pay for utilities, but the rent was based on my mom's income. So, no matter how much my mom made, she would be left with roughly the same meager amount of money after living expenses were taken care of, and that wasn't ever enough.

My mother had no degrees or certifications, so she couldn't get a higher-paying job. However, she had learned how to type, so she used a temporary job agency to help her find work. This helped a little when she got an assignment, but getting a job meant her monthly food stamps and welfare benefits decreased, while the monthly rent increased.

People think that going on food stamps and welfare is a free ride to an easy life, but once you get stuck in that system, it's difficult to escape. Furthermore, government assistance is not a lifeboat that will float forever. Recipients eventually exhaust their benefits, and after that, eviction comes. If you get evicted from the projects, your options are either staying with family or becoming homeless.

As a result of this dynamic, most people in the projects take up side hustles that the government doesn't tax, like babysitting, drug dealing, or selling "40s"—forty-ounce glass bottles of malt liquor. My mom dabbled in all three at different times, but she also used another tactic to lessen the financial burden: She got a boyfriend living with her but kept him off the lease.

Just Because It's Normal Doesn't Mean It's Right

I don't remember how my mom met Fred. I just remember he appeared one day and started living with us. He worked at Wendy's and liked to build model airplanes. He would occasionally play me in *Tecmo Super Bowl* on my Nintendo, but other than that, I don't have any positive memories of him.

Instead, I remember the beatings. Aside from striking us with a belt or extension cord, Fred would make us put our hands against the wall, extend our arms, and kick out our feet so that our arms were the only thing keeping us from falling to the ground. Then we'd have to hold the pose indefinitely. He beat us if we bent our arms or dropped to a knee. I grew up thinking these types of beatings from Fred were normal for two tragic reasons: Everyone around me received similar beatings, and my mom often beat me worse.

The popular saying was "A hard head makes a soft ass," meaning, kids who don't listen got beat. It's the ghetto version of "Spare the rod, spoil the child." The problem with beating young children is that they can't make the connection between the pain and what they did wrong. It only makes them fearful of the adults around them. This type of punishment doesn't teach a kid anything but how to be afraid, and it sets them up for failure later in life.

Even if children could make the connection, beating them doesn't teach them anything about how to behave correctly. It only teaches them that violence is the way to get what they want. Proponents of physical discipline often call them "spankings," but at least in the hood, we didn't grow up with any illusions. Everyone I grew up with called these acts exactly what they were.

We weren't spanked. We were beaten. "Spanking" sounds harmless and innocent. When you hear "spanking," you think of someone putting a young child over their lap for a few open-palmed slaps to teach them the error of their ways. Worst case, the image that comes to mind is of the child being hit across the ass a few times with a belt. That is not what I experienced, nor was it the experience of many children I grew up around.

My sister and I were beaten with everything from belts and extension cords to plastic bats and, as we got older, open-handed slaps and plastic hangers. Once, my mom was pissed that I hadn't cleaned up my room, so she started throwing all the stuff at me that I hadn't picked up. One of those things was a snow boot, and she launched it with all the fury of an out-of-control woman under the heavy influence of alcohol. It landed squarely on my brow and opened a cut that I should have gotten stitched up, but my mom wasn't going to take me to the hospital for a wound she had inflicted.

Whenever people asked what happened, I told them that I hurt myself during a "rock fight" with the neighborhood kids. This wasn't unbelievable, as I often had rock fights with other boys as a game. It was a dangerously stupid way to pass the time, but it was fun. We were all used to getting beat up at home, so getting tagged with a few boulders while talking shit never seemed like a big deal to us. Of course, when you play stupid games, you win stupid prizes.

Play Stupid Games, Win Stupid Prizes

One day, my mom sent me to a corner store, and I crossed paths with some kids I had tossed rocks with before. This time, they decided to take things to the next level and tried to jump me. There were four of them, but it's hard for prepubescent kids to do real damage to each other—at least with their bare hands. In the middle of me dancing around, throwing blows at one kid and evading another, one of the kids I wasn't fending off picked up a rock. He launched a stone the size of my fist from a distance that was far enough for him to get a good windup and too close for me to dodge it. It landed square on my eyebrow, busting it open.

It must have been severe, because it didn't hurt, and lack of feeling is a telltale sign of damage. (Part of that is the adrenaline rush, the fight-or-flight survival response.) The other telltale sign was that instead of continuing the harassment, the kids took one look at me and fled the scene of the crime. I continued to the corner store, not wanting to disobey my mother.

"Yo, kid, you're bleeding pretty bad."

"I'm OK, man."

"Aight, whatever."

The corner-store guy sold me a box of cornstarch, and I staggered home, where my mom took one look at me and rushed me to the hospital for stitches. When we got back, she and Fred got into it. It turned out the kids who attacked me were the children of the woman Fred was seeing on the side. My mom knew about the affair but stayed with Fred anyway, which infuriated the other woman. She'd instructed her kids to beat me up when they saw me. That day, as I passed their apartment row, they finally acted on her orders.

Aside from beating the hell out of my sister and me and indirectly landing me in the hospital, Fred was also a criminal. My sister and I often accompanied my mom to visit him at the county jail. I remember waiting in a narrow hallway before we were let past the bars, guarded by correctional officers, so we could sit and she could talk to Fred.

I don't know what Fred got locked up in county jail so often for, but I remember being happy whenever he was away, and I hated it when he was back home. I don't understand why, but he somehow made my mom happy. She sent him money for a commissary in jail and accepted his collect calls. (If you've never received a collect call, the recipient of those calls has to pay for them.) We sure didn't have the money, but somehow, she found the funds to help pay for this loser in jail.

He also cost us money when he wasn't in jail. I remember one day when my mother got the phone bill, and there were over two hundred dollars in charges from calls to 1-900 sex chat lines. Back in the days before OnlyFans and streaming internet porn, guys had fewer options to satisfy their needs, extramarital or otherwise.

Men could call these chat lines and talk dirty to women for $4.99 a minute. Just like the porn of today, these chat lines were addictive. Unlike the porn of today, they were not free.

The commercials for these lines ran overnight on television, and I'm sure there were ads in adult video stores as well. As a five-year-old, I was neither up overnight nor had I ever been in an adult video store, but when my mom confronted Fred about the bill, he tried to say that I was making those calls. My mom might have been stupidly in love, but she wasn't stupid enough to believe that.

Despite her many flaws, my mom never tolerated physical abuse from Fred. So, when he hit her during this argument, she struck back, and they started fighting right over the ironing board where he was prepping his Wendy's uniform. At five foot nine and around two hundred pounds, my mom was a force to be reckoned with, especially against Fred, who was small—maybe 165 pounds soaking wet after a big meal. They shoved, exchanged blows, and shouted, but in the end, she threw him out.

Unfortunately, it wasn't the last time we'd see Fred. My mom—a woman who tolerated her man's cheating and her child being attacked by his mistress's kids—was not about to be deterred by a phone-sex bill higher than our rent, or even by domestic abuse. When Fred came back a few days later, they made up, and for a short while, things seemed OK.

I imagine part of the reason my mom tolerated Fred is that she viewed him as a better alternative to the crackheads across the hall who would sometimes babysit us. Since Fred worked the closing shifts at Wendy's, from 3:00 to 11:00 p.m., he was available to babysit during the day.

When I was five, I was old enough to attend kindergarten while my two-year-old sister stayed home with Fred. One day, when I got home, I found her in tears.

"Jasmine! Tell your brother what you did," Fred yelled at her.

"I . . . I broke your train." Between her toddler level of speech and her crying, I could hardly understand what she was saying to me.

"Now you hit her for that shit," Fred barked at me. I'd been beaten before, but my mom never made us hit each other. Hitting my sister was something that would almost guarantee an ass-whooping from my mom, but Fred was the adult in charge, so I hit her in the arm.

Fred then dropped us off downstairs with a neighbor, Ms. Tiny, while he got ready for work. I always thought it was funny that we called her Ms. Tiny, because she was severely overweight. Anyway, she took one look at the bleeding welts on my sister and knew something was wrong.

"Oh damn, he fucked her up good," said Ms. Tiny's boyfriend. "We heard that shit earlier and wondered what the hell was happening." Ms. Tiny and her boyfriend now realized the screams they had heard coming from upstairs earlier that day were the result of a grown man beating a toddler with a metal coat hanger.

After Ms. Tiny called my mom, she then called one of her nephews, a known gang member.

"If you see him, fuck him up," she told him. "Beatin' on a baby like this is fucked up."

The thing was, I'd heard Ms. Tiny beat *her* kids, so if she thought it warranted street justice, it must have been bad. But I didn't expect anyone to do anything. My world had already taught me that no one really cared about helping others. If my parents couldn't handle threats to their own children, why would I expect random thugs to help? Everyone around me had their own problems, and even as a kid, I knew being a problem just brought the wrong kind of attention.

Hard Lessons About Life Are Learned, Not Taught

My father was a nonfactor in my life. He wasn't a deadbeat, exactly: He paid child support and sent me gifts for my birthday and Christmas. He even took me to the beach and skiing a few times. I was probably the only kid in the ghetto who could ski, and that was because my dad took me. However, when I think of my father, I'm not left with anything besides those gifts.

I don't remember my dad ever living in the same city as me, since he moved to Philadelphia shortly after I was born. I spoke to him on the phone once or twice a month, but aside from two summers spent with him, I saw him only once a year, when he visited Pittsburgh. Occasionally, if he had a compelling reason—not related to his children—I might get to see him twice in a year.

He was neither someone I wanted to be like nor someone I despised. I didn't feel loved by him, nor did I feel abandoned. He never helped me with anything, but he never hurt me either. He was neither strict nor lenient. When he died, I cried from natural emotion, but I did not miss him, because there was no relationship or memories to long for.

I understand that things could have been worse. I knew many kids who never even met their fathers. These kids were raised by single mothers in the truest sense; there was no financial support, no phone calls or Christmas gifts. Those children never saw their father—once a year or otherwise. But just because I knew my father didn't mean he was around to protect my sister and me.

My father criticized my mom for us living in the projects, and for drinking and smoking weed, but he didn't do anything to change that situation: He moved three hundred miles away and kept his distance for most of my life. Still, I got to see my father. I didn't know him, but I got to see him. My dad would pick me up once or twice a year and lug me around for the day while visiting friends before returning me to my mother.

My mom was on her own, and that meant making some tough choices to help raise her children. For money, mom got connected with selling 40s and weed. She started leaving my sister with relatives so she could work, and I got a key to let myself in after school. My strict instructions were never to open the door for anyone. She didn't need to tell me twice, as I had already seen enough to know that our world was dangerous.

One day, as I walked to my school bus stop, a woman burst out of her apartment, hysterical and tearful. Behind her, a ragged man chased after her, shouting, "Bitch, where the fuck do you think you're going?!" He quickly caught up, shoved her down, and began beating her with a tree branch. Her nose was bloody, and she screamed for him to stop. Instead of intervening or offering help, the other adults in the street hurried their children along to the bus stop.

"Mind ya business."

"Shit, that's between him and her."

"Keep ya ass walkin'. Don't want no parts of that shit."

As they walked away, the adults were careful to not even look in the direction of this open display of violence. Some of the older kids, already familiar with the harsh rules of the world, didn't have to be told to act like nothing was happening. Children are naturally curious, but curiosity in an environment like that could get you into serious trouble.

We lived in Terrace Village until I was ten. When those housing projects were set to be demolished and rebuilt, residents were relocated to other housing projects in the city. My family ended up across town, in the Northview Heights Estates housing project. Despite the regal-sounding name, there was nothing luxurious about the place.

Northview Heights was a gated community, but that gate had been erected to keep tabs on the residents and their visitors, in an attempt to decrease the presence of violence and drugs. It didn't work, but the gate was a symbol.

The gate wasn't there to protect the residents from outside influences. It was there to keep the influence of Northview Heights from infecting the rest of the city.

Don't Get Outworked by a Crackhead

When I was five, during one of my dad's visits, he parked the car and pulled out a red-and-silver metal device he proceeded to lock around the steering wheel. My curiosity was instantly piqued.

"Hey, dad," I asked. "What's that?"

"It's the Club."

"Why are you putting it on your car?"

"So some crackhead doesn't steal my car and sell it for five dollars."

For those not familiar with the Club, it's essentially an oversized bicycle lock. It attaches to a vehicle's steering wheel, making it impossible to turn, even while it's on. It was a popular anti-theft device in the 1980s and '90s, but you don't see it too often today, as the marketing for car alarms and the false sense of security created by radio frequency keys took it out of style.

I laughed, but my father's response confused me. While my five-year-old self didn't know the exact price of a car, I knew they cost a lot more than five dollars. I'd also seen my neighbors smoke crack and shoot heroin. Still, I didn't know anything about crackheads other than the fact that they were skinny and had poor hygiene. When my mom was in a playful mood, she'd threaten to give my sister and me to a crackhead who would sell us for fifty dollars.

I started to understand something about crack addicts: They didn't operate by the rules that other people did. They had their own prices, their own rules—and they all revolved around getting crack. But when we moved to Northview Heights, my next-door neighbor was no longer just an addict. Instead, I now had the unique experience of living next to a drug dealer.

The houses in Northview Heights were row houses, so you shared a wall and a porch with your next-door neighbor. We happened to share this wall and porch with a "trap house"—just another name for a place where drugs are sold. Selling drugs isn't like most businesses, and when you live next to someone involved in that line of work, you become painfully aware of that fact. There's a good reason why the late Notorious B.I.G. warned in "Ten Crack Commandments" to "never sell no crack where you rest at."

First, there were the hours. Crackheads seem to function on a circadian rhythm that's the opposite of most people's; given the low police presence in the projects, it's not like crackheads have some practical reason for only visiting the trap house after the sun goes down. When you share a wall with someone, you can hear any time they have a visitor who knocks on the door. Most nights, from dusk until dawn, the house next to me was a crack convenience store.

I remember walking to the bus stop once with my mother. It was so early that the sun had barely started to come up. We turned the corner to the bus stop, and a man started walking in our direction, but like he was coming directly toward us.

I was scared, but my mom continued walking without hesitation. I took my mom's lead; I didn't even make eye contact. He scurried past us as if we didn't even exist. Once he passed, my mom shook her head and blurted out, "I been watching that same dope fiend out here chasing a high all day and night for three damn days."

This always stuck with me because I couldn't imagine staying up for three days straight for anything. Even when I tried to stay up late playing video games, the longest I could make it was 2:00 a.m.—maybe 3:00 a.m. if I was really in the zone and didn't have school the next day. However, by that point in my life, I had enough experience with crackheads to know that this was most likely not an exaggeration.

Then there was the collateral damage that came with living next to a crack house. The problems linked to drugs are often not caused by the users themselves. While someone going through withdrawal—"fiendin'," it's called—is certainly more likely to rob you, drug users are generally not violent criminals. A U.S. Department of Justice (USDOJ) report titled "Drug Use, Dependence, and Abuse Among State Prisoners and Jail Inmates, 2007–2009" reports that only 14 percent of those incarcerated for violent crime committed the offense for money to buy drugs.

Of course, 14 percent is not zero. Crackheads do commit armed robbery. When I was twelve, a crackhead materialized out of thin air while I was letting myself into my dad's apartment. He held me up at knifepoint for the calzone my dad had sent me out to pick up. After he checked my pockets for any money I might have, he said, "Thanks, man. Good looking out," and vanished just as effortlessly as he had appeared. At least he had good manners.

A crackhead is far more likely, however, to break into your house. The same report by the U.S. Department of Justice revealed that 39 percent of people jailed for crimes of property theft committed them to get money for drugs.

Crackheads will steal anything that isn't bolted down, operating under the belief that everything has a "street value." The crackhead believes that if someone paid money for it once, they'll pay money for it again. As a crackhead is not typically living for the future, they don't preemptively steal and load up a reserve of money for future drug purchases. For example, when I was twenty-one, a crackhead once broke into the apartment I shared with friends and stole only a jar of change and our cable box. He by-passed a valuable PlayStation 2, driven solely by his need for money to get high. His desperation led him to take only the items that would most immediately feed his addiction, leaving the rest behind.

The thing that's most strongly etched in my memory about living next to this drug dealer wasn't the frequent door knocks throughout the night or the occasional break-ins, though. It was the violence. Not the violence against users, or other dealers—the violence against his girlfriend.

Hearing his customers knock at the door during all hours of the night wasn't even that bad. Very often, they'd knock on our door by mistake. And even then, if someone was awake to hear it, all you had to shout was "Next door," or "Wrong house," and they got the message. But on the nights when business was slow, the dealer beat the living hell out of this poor woman. I've witnessed a lot of violence in my life, but there is something uniquely disturbing about only hearing it—especially when it's not an even fight. I could hear the pain and fear in the woman's screams just as easily as I could hear the sounds of his blows.

The type of person willing to attack a woman like this has no qualms about attacking someone else's children either. Once, my sister played a prank that resulted in this guy being hit with an egg. In response, he chased her to our back door and tried to push his way inside. I pushed him back so hard that he fell over, and for the rest of that summer, I lived in fear that he was going to shoot me.

I've met dealers of all different substances. My general experience has been that the harder the drug, the worse the human being is that deals it. Maybe it's a result of the ruthlessness you need to get into and survive the game. Harder drugs are worth more money, so the competition is tougher, and it requires a more dangerous person to succeed. It's not like you beat the competition by running a better ad campaign. On the street, you eliminate the competition the same way you'd take out a bunch of ants trying to make off with your food.

Even when I was a little kid, I had few illusions about the harsh realities of the world and how people behaved when survival was at stake. But moving to Northview Heights and attending school there revealed to me a new level of ruthlessness. In that neighborhood, nearly everyone seemed touched by a raw, survival-driven edge that was far more intense than anything I had previously encountered.

II

If You Can't Beat Your Environment, Change It

"Stop crying before I give you something to cry about!"

My mom would shout that phrase at my sister and me *after* she had already beaten us. As I got older, and my mother could no longer easily use physical violence to control me, she resorted to fear and emotional manipulation. One Easter, she lost a dime bag of marijuana, and believing that one of us had thrown it in the garbage, she decided to throw out all of our candy as a punishment. If she needed something, and I didn't respond fast enough, or my effort wasn't to her satisfaction, she would say in her angriest and most sarcastic tone, "I didn't need your help anyway."

My mother loved us like all mothers love their children, but her approach to raising us was subpar. She set a horrible example with her behavior and then severely chastised us when we copied the behavior she had modeled. I eventually learned that the best way to win this game was not to play it at all.

Parents often justify hitting their children as a way to teach them a lesson, but my mother's approach was more about venting her anger than instilling discipline. She'd beat us not to correct our behavior but to release her own frustration; the angrier she was, the harsher the beating. Our pain was irrelevant; what mattered was how quickly she could find relief from her rage. The beatings would only stop when she felt better, regardless of whether they left us barely touched or in severe pain, requiring us to invent stories for teachers about bruises and swelling.

But it wasn't just my mom who I had to worry about. The terms "bullying" and "teasing" whitewash the trauma of my childhood. On buses, in hallways, walking to and from school—violence waited for me around every corner. Tormentors hounded me, latching on to any excuse to escalate verbal taunting into physical assault.

Whether it was on the school bus, in the schoolyard, or around the neighborhood, there was always someone harassing me, and that harassment usually led to a physical confrontation. Fending off attacks from classmates or street toughs became a daily, exhausting norm, and the damage inflicted went beyond cuts and bruises. I spent my childhood constantly in fight-or-flight mode, wondering when and from what direction the next attack would come.

My psyche was fighting a battle on two fronts. Domestically, I dealt with the emotional instability and physical abuse of my mother. At school, I fought off my bullies. And to make matters worse, my neighborhood was a literal war zone. The sound of gunshots was a regular occurrence during the night, and during the day, the elementary school I went to had gang-fire-shooting drills. Later, my middle school enacted a uniform policy to reduce the visible evidence of gang affiliation. The only way I kept myself sane was to retreat into my mind and focus on the things I had control over.

You Can't Control How You Feel— But You Can Control How You React

As a child, I couldn't do anything about where I lived or who I went to school with. I couldn't control the behavior of my mom or other kids. I was born into unfortunate circumstances that came with significant risk, but there was nothing I could do about it. I could only control how I lived, thought, and behaved.

The Serenity Prayer, associated with Alcoholics Anonymous and other twelve-step programs, captures this idea in a beautifully poetic fashion. The prayer goes as follows:

> *God, grant me the serenity to accept the things I cannot change,*
> *Courage to change the things I can,*
> *And wisdom to know the difference.*

The prayer is a reminder not to worry about things one cannot control, to take action on things within one's power to affect, and to recognize which is which. That last line is key. You can waste a lot of time and energy trying to change things that aren't yours to change, no matter how much you work at it. While you're engaged in those pointless battles, you're depleting resources that could impact those aspects of your life that would yield to your efforts if you could only see them.

This viewpoint is identical to "the dichotomy of control." The dichotomy of control is a crucial concept in Stoic philosophy that distinguishes between what we can and cannot control. The Stoics argued that much of our unhappiness stems from trying to exert control over things that are not within our power. For example, we cannot control other people's opinions or behavior, political outcomes, health diagnoses, or natural disasters. Focusing our emotions and desires on external things leads to frustration, anxiety, anger, and disappointment.

The Stoics maintain that we should focus our time and energy on what is within our power—but to do that, you must first realize that you have no control over almost anything. Once you understand that, you focus on the only things you control: your judgments, values, desires, and actions. As the Stoic philosopher Epictetus said, "Some things are up to us, and some things are not up to us."

Please notice what I did not list under "what we can control": I can't control how I *feel* about something or someone. Hurtful things said and done to me in my childhood still caused me pain and sadness. I still got angry at the people who did me harm. I couldn't control that, but I could control my behavior toward them.

Growing up in a violent neighborhood reinforced the value of remaining levelheaded, even when tensions ran high. In places like the hood where people have few material possessions, respect is paramount, and conflicts can quickly escalate when someone feels disrespected. Although I had several fights as a child, I avoided many more by simply apologizing.

In neighborhoods wracked by violence, it's the idea of honor that often leads to conflict. Honor refers to a form of status tied to integrity and character, which is not something you'd typically associate with street life. In this sense, it's more related to the idea of reputation. In neighborhoods like the poverty-stricken public housing projects I grew up in, one's willingness to use physical force to defend their reputation against insult or challenge is what matters.

If you're like most people, using physical violence in response to words seems absurd. But you must remember that people will always find something to take pride in, no matter how little they might seem to have to be proud of. If you're last in the pecking order, your reputation among the other people at that level may be the only thing you have to take pride in. In that case, you just can't let someone talk to—or about—you in a disrespectful manner.

Saying "my bad" went a long way in keeping an accidental brush on a crowded bus from turning into an all-out brawl. Even if the other person was wrong, swallowing my pride prevented countless unnecessary fights that could have ended badly.

People respond better to humility and respect, even amid chaos. Good manners and emotional control never make a situation worse. Staying disciplined with my emotions granted me inner resilience and social capital that have paid dividends throughout my life. The ability to rein in your feelings and see beyond surface provocations is powerful in any environment, not just one where you can get hurt or even killed.

When School Is Like a Prison, the Students Behave Like Inmates

Understanding that I had the power to shape my own destiny—that what ultimately happened to me was controlled by my beliefs, choices, and actions rather than by the hand of fate—kept me from becoming a victim to my environment. However, I still made mistakes, but the penalties for those mistakes became more severe as I got older.

Likeability only goes so far. Sometimes, it even motivates someone to attack you, so they can elevate their social status by trying to degrade yours. Middle school is where I learned how to survive and stand up for myself—because not only was no one coming to save me, it felt like everyone was coming to *get* me.

Kids went to school based on the part of the city they lived in. This meant that unless you were in a special academic program, your elementary, middle, and high schools were determined based on your address. I went to Allegheny Middle School (AMS), one of the feeder schools for most of the projects and low-income neighborhoods in Pittsburgh's North Side.

AMS was full of other kids from my housing project. It was also the feeder school for the Allegheny Commons, Spring Hill, and Fineview housing projects, along with two other gang-affiliated neighborhoods, Manchester and the Mexican War Streets. The school also had a few poor white kids from the working-class neighborhoods of Troy Hill and Spring Garden.

The administrators of Pittsburgh Public Schools (PPS) believed this demographic mixture could be explosive, so they put in three hedges to quell any potential violence: We had to wear uniforms of khaki bottoms and white shirts, there were armed police officers on duty for security, and we had to pass through metal detectors on our way into school every day. A few other elementary and middle schools in the city had uniforms, and a few high schools had police officers and metal detectors, but my middle school was the first to hit the trifecta. I guess they figured that elementary school was too young to require metal detectors and armed security, and high schoolers would resist a uniform with great fervor, but middle schoolers were just right—young enough to accept restrictions on our self-expression but, given our circumstances and backgrounds, old enough to use that self-expression for nefarious purposes if permitted.

What school administrators hoped to accomplish with the uniforms and metal detectors was simple enough: If everyone wore the same thing, they figured, kids wouldn't be able to divide themselves by the colors of their neighborhood gangs. I knew kids in middle school who had older siblings in gangs, but it turns out that, contrary to what you might think, middle school isn't too young to be in a gang yourself. In 1996, the year these changes hit my middle school, an Office of Justice survey found that 16 percent of gang members were younger than fifteen, and a 2014 study showed that the typical gang member joins at age thirteen but only remains active until age fifteen. This is the time when most of us in the United

States are in middle school, so it makes sense that the Pittsburgh schools' intervention initiatives would be targeted at that group. And just in case the uniforms didn't work out, there were the metal detectors. And if those didn't work out, hopefully the police officers on the premises would ensure there wasn't a problem.

But these measures also made the school feel like a prison. We all dressed the same, ate at the same time, and passed through gray metal boxes each day before we were deemed safe enough to enter our classrooms. And if these interventions were meant to improve our conduct, they failed miserably. Just because they took away our external differences didn't mean that we wouldn't find other reasons to disagree. Just because we couldn't bring our own weapons didn't mean that we wouldn't find other ways to hurt each other. Just because security was there didn't mean that we wouldn't try to fight. Little learning took place in that school because of the constant behavior disruptions.

If you treat kids like they belong in prison, they're going to live up to your expectations. Middle school was where I first started to understand a hard truth, but one that would eventually move me to take the first step toward altering my life: Sometimes you can't beat your environment—and in that case, you've got to change it.

Bullies Want an Easy Target— Not a Real Fight

I was bullied—a lot. Other kids thought that I looked like a gorilla; from the fourth grade, my nickname was "Congo," after the best-selling Michael Crichton novel about apes that was adapted into a 1995 movie.

It was called "ripping" when I was growing up, because we ripped into each other about our respective flaws and issues. These were often exaggerated for comedic effect. While I never let taunts and teasing goad me into being the first to throw blows, I learned that if you give people an inch, they'll try to take a mile. And occasionally, you'd say something that made a kid extra angry because you struck a sensitive subject in his life. Once, in the seventh grade, this kid made a joke about my grandma. In return, I said something about his. His grandmother was dead, so he took it personally, and a fight ensued.

This incident always stuck in my memory because it was the first time I realized that psychological bullying operates with the same dynamic as physical bullying. In both types, the bully doesn't really want a fight. They want a punching bag to take out their insecurities and frustrations on, because they believe that bringing someone down can make them feel better about themselves. The moment you fight back, you remind them of their inadequacy and powerlessness. This is why your dealings with bullies always escalate. How you respond doesn't matter; one way or the other, the taunting and teasing always becomes a full-blown confrontation. It doesn't matter whether you ignore them or rip them back with greater vitriol: The harassment never stops at words.

If a fight occurred at school, being the first one to swing meant that you'd be the one to receive the punishment. It didn't matter how much you were provoked or the nature of the provocation. If you swung first, you were the one who got suspended. During the same seventh-grade year, this kid who was hassling me broke into my locker and threw my coat in an unflushed toilet. To make matters worse, it was the middle of January. When I went looking for my coat at the end of the day, some kids tipped me off where it was and who had put it there. In my opinion, I was perfectly justified in delivering a beatdown the next day. The principal disagreed, and I received a three-day suspension from school. However, on the bright side, none of my belongings ended up in the toilet again.

This incident reveals another thing about the nature of fights in school. You couldn't wait to take action; otherwise, it would look unprovoked, and the school administration would treat you as the aggressor. I remember a kid throwing food at me all week. I kept ignoring him, but every day, I had to go home and wash one of my two white shirts. My mom finally got tired of me washing my shirts every day and wasting her money on laundry. To avoid a beating from her, I had to dish one out myself. It worked—the chicken stopped flying at me during lunch. But since he hadn't technically hit me first on the day I went after him, I ended up with an extra three-day suspension.

Administrative Punishment Does Not Fix Behavior That Is Socially Rewarded

It's not like suspensions were a serious punishment. I looked at them like vacation days. While I didn't go out of my way to get suspended, I did not understand the logic of forbidding a child to go to school as a punishment. Perhaps, if your parents were heavily involved in your life, they would punish you for getting suspended. But most kids who frequently got suspended lived with single moms who, even if they did care, couldn't do anything about it because they had to work during the day.

What else was the school supposed to do? A big problem with inner-city schools that are rife with disruptive behavior is that most kids aren't troublemakers—the ones that do cause trouble cause *almost all* of the trouble. It's an exaggerated Pareto distribution, where 5 percent of students account for 99 percent of the suspensions. The problem with suspensions, however, is they don't fix anything. I know this because I was suspended from school at least fifteen times. Giving me time off from school was anything but a punishment. I slept in, played my two favorite video games— *Final Fantasy VII* and *Xenogears*—and watched TV. School suspensions didn't exempt you from schoolwork that was due on the days you were out, but I never cared much about that because middle school was easy.

For some children, suspensions from school do make their lives worse. We were poor kids who relied on the school breakfast and lunch program for sufficient caloric intake. When you're suspended, this gets taken away. Other kids were dealing with abuse at home, and school was their only reprieve from hell. Ironically, kids in these conditions are exactly the type of kids who are more likely to act in a way that will get them suspended.

The other issue is that getting suspended was a badge of honor. The type of kid who got suspended was likely having a hard time in school already, and it becomes even more difficult to learn and perform well when you're missing days. So, what do you do? You embrace being part of a group of misfits. Kids are always looking for a group to belong to. After being rejected from school, dealing with domestic issues, having their self-esteem battered by failures, and being told they're delinquent, they fall into the only crowd willing to accept them: other kids who are in the same boat. And then everybody sinks together.

When the Fight Is Everywhere, There's Nowhere to Hide

Fights in Northview Heights were different than fights at school. The problem with fighting in your neighborhood was that there were no security guards or metal detectors. This meant that the violence not only was more intense but had the potential to last a lot longer.

Once, I got into a fight with some kids at a summer day camp hosted by the neighborhood. Like the bullies at school, none of them could take it as well as they could dish it out, and when I started to rip them back, they didn't like it. However, unlike at school, there were no restraints on what they could use as a weapon.

They chased me down until they had me cornered. Instead of picking up the usual assortment of stones, bricks, or sticks that were frequently used as ghetto weapons, one of them grabbed an empty beer bottle and broke off the end like we were in some bar fight. I'd only seen this done in the movies, but this kid had his technique down. He turned that twenty-ounce glass bottle of Coors Light into a jagged-edged weapon.

The kid was bigger than me, and I didn't see a clear way around him. He was angry because when it comes to "ripping," I had crossed the one line you never cross, insulting the person that you only insult when you are definitely looking for a fight. It wasn't his mother—"yo momma" jokes were in every kid's repertoire in the nineties. A few sensitive souls took them to heart or used them as an excuse to fight, but most of us didn't take them seriously.

He said something messed up about me, and in return, I said, "Ya dead folks, nigga."

It didn't matter who had started the battle—referencing someone's deceased relatives was an open invitation to finish it. If it was just the two of you, they might let it slide. But I'd retaliated this way in front of other kids who knew the rules. This meant he *had* to do something.

Fortunately, I managed to talk him down. I was equally skilled at talking myself out of trouble as talking myself into it, but this was a close call. It's not like I would have gone to the police if he had cut me with that bottle. My only recourse would have been to try to get back at him, starting a feud that would have continued until one of us was seriously hurt or killed. This might sound extreme for kids, but this was our reality.

Another difference between fighting in the neighborhood and fighting at school was that in the neighborhood, there was no statute of limitations on getting revenge. No one was worried about getting suspended if they waited to retaliate. After I'd been picked on incessantly that summer, my mother walked me up to the play-ground and called out everyone who was picking on me. She then lined us up to fight it out.

It's already embarrassing enough to have your mother pick fights on your behalf, but it'd be even worse if I lost. In retrospect, I have conflicted feelings about what she did. On the one hand, letting kids fight out their problems in a bare-knuckle fashion seems barbaric. Even if they don't pick up a stick, brick, or glass bottle, it's an easy way for a kid to get serious injuries: cuts deep enough to require stitches, fractures, or concussions. We were preteens, not even finished with puberty, so no one was really strong enough to break eye sockets, but there were still risks.

On the other hand, this was as close to a sanctioned bout as you could get on the streets. It was called "getting a fair one." The adults were old school, so they didn't mind a fair fight. With onlookers, you were usually safe from someone picking up a weapon or jumping in. Both were a constant danger, but with the adults watching, it typically never got to that point.

After my mom made me fight three kids in a row, the rest of my tormentors lost their taste for battle. It was a relief, because I was getting exhausted, and number four would have kicked my ass. But the gauntlet of fights stopped my harassment in the neighborhood. After the conflict had been settled physically, there was nothing else to do. A lot of these kids either became my friends or at least stopped bothering me. However, it didn't always turn out that way.

Once, I got into a conflict with a kid and his friends who started throwing rocks at me while I was minding my business, playing in the mud. Of course, I made sure that I fired back. I hit one of the kids, and a bunch of shit-talking ensued about how they were gonna kick my ass and bring an entire audience to watch. I didn't believe them, so I just kept talking shit.

Later that night, there was a knock on my door. About twenty people had gathered in front of my house, and some teenage girl was daring me to come outside to fight her. I was courageous, but I wasn't stupid. The crowd was chanting for me to come outside, throwing rocks and bottles, fully expecting me to emerge.

The incident didn't escalate, but I know that had I stepped outside, it wouldn't have just been me against this teenage girl who decided to be a champion for her cousins. I would have likely been jumped and beaten into a coma by a bunch of strangers.

Of all the fights I had, the details of one stand out in my memory. It was a fight that almost ruined my young life before it got started.

Ignorance of the Law Doesn't Protect You from the Consequences of Breaking It

I learned about the "Crackhead Hustle" from firsthand experience and observation. But I never sold drugs, though drug dealing was always around me. The closest I ever got to selling drugs was once in the eighth grade, when I thought it would be hilarious to bring a bag of sugar to school and pretend I was selling cocaine.

Some of the kids had far more experience with hard drugs than I did and immediately recognized a fake. "Shit, that ain't real," one of my classmates said. "Coke don't even look like that." Others, however, had a stronger reaction to my joke.

"Nigga, don't try to sell me no shit like that. Just wait till after class. I'm fuckin' you up." Even in eighth grade, Dennis was six feet tall and easily weighed 250 pounds. He was built like an offensive lineman. He was one of the few kids bigger than me, and he already didn't like me. I never knew why, but I knew he wasn't a fan. Dennis had bullied a few other kids, but he had never made a move on me directly; I imagine he wasn't sure exactly how that would turn out for him. Well, my drug prank finally pushed him over the edge.

The fight was epic. Tables were flipped; desks were thrown. Dennis used his forty-pound weight advantage to slam me to the ground with ease. While this fight started as your typical schoolhouse brawl, it quickly deteriorated into a street fight, and so each of us invoked the rules of the street to survive. One of the most important rules is "Don't get on the ground," because there, you're easy to kick and stomp, and you can't throw any punches to defend yourself.

To prevent him from lying on top of me, I immediately sat up and, from the awkward sitting position I had maneuvered into, unloaded a barrage of punches to his groin. So by the time I got to my feet, Dennis had remembered another rule of street fighting: "Pick up *anything* and use it as a weapon." My punches to the groin angered him to the point where he was capable of hurling the classroom's overhead projector at me like a missile. Luckily, I managed to dodge it and keep fighting until the school police officers broke us up and escorted us individually to the principal's office.

After hearing what the fight was about, the police officers took me to a separate room.

"We gotta arrest you."

"Wait, what? It wasn't really coke. It was just sugar."

"You tried to sell a cosmetic look-alike. We gotta arrest you like you were selling the real thing. Now, don't make this difficult. Put your hands behind your back."

"I didn't know that selling fake sugar like it's cocaine is against the law!"

"Ignorance of the law doesn't protect you from the consequences of breaking it."

Until that moment, my only fear about this whole thing was the ass-kicking my mom would give me for trying to sell sugar as cocaine. Now, I was worried about going to Shuman Juvenile Detention Center because I had simulated the sale of a controlled substance. I thought about all the stories I'd heard about guys getting raped in jail.

The officers put me in the back of the police van, and so began the end of my life.

After about five minutes, we stopped on the side of the road, and one of the officers climbed into the back of the wagon with me. He undid the cuffs and began teaching me a valuable lesson.

"If you pulled that shit on the street, someone woulda shot you. You can't just start selling drugs—especially fake ones."

"I was just making a joke. I didn't know it would start a fight. I'm always making jokes about drugs."

"I don't know why that kid got so mad, but it could have been a lot worse for you. You better not forget this."

The officers then drove me home.

I had been around drug dealers and drug users all my life, but I didn't know how the game worked. I just thought it might be funny to pretend to sell coke. Luckily for me, these officers decided to use the incident to teach me a lesson instead of putting another kid into the system. I don't know how my life would have turned out had they actually processed my arrest, but the statistics on the matter tell me that the officers' decision that day kept me from a life spent in and out of jail. That lesson stayed with me.

Dennis got a three-day suspension. I got nothing, despite being the one who had violated an actual law. However, at the time, I wished I had gotten suspended, because the swelling of my face and lips ignited even more jokes about my appearance.

Later, I did some research to see if the officer who spoke to me was bluffing. He wasn't: Under Pennsylvania law, the offense is called "simulated controlled substance possession" or "simulated controlled substance delivery." It is a misdemeanor of the second degree, which can result in penalties including imprisonment, fines, or both. The penalties may vary depending on the circumstances and the individual's intent.

I got lucky that day. My penalty was being scared into being a law-abiding citizen.

Change Your Life Before
Your Life Changes You

Both in school and back in the hood, fighting was miserable, but the worst place to fight was during the journey between the two places: on the school bus. Many incidents that took place on the school bus blur together, but one stands out in my memory because of how dangerous it was. It was a bus ride home like any other, which meant that a fight broke out. Fights didn't always happen, but they happened often enough that you came to expect some type of disruption on your ride home, even if it wasn't a fight. Kids were also notorious for launching objects at the bus drivers, and some of them started fights with the drivers. A few bus drivers had even been fired for engaging with these student attacks, though you couldn't really blame them.

However, one day, while we were on I-279 north, the highway we'd sometimes take home from school, all hell broke loose. A fight turned into an all-out brawl. Someone began hurling pencils at the bus driver. A fire was started in the back of the bus and, to put it out, the kids decided it was a good idea to open the rear emergency exit door while the bus was speeding down the freeway at sixty miles per hour.

My mother always used to say to me, "God protects babies and fools." What she meant by this was that you only survived doing stupid stuff because there must be some type of divine intervention at play. I got off the bus that day thinking about how lucky I was that I was still breathing. Sure, the fights at school and in the neighborhood had been bad, but I was reasonably confident that I could survive them. At that moment, however, I knew that I had to figure out something different for my transportation, because I wasn't sure I could survive *this*. If I was going to die before making it to high school, I was convinced that it was going to be in a school bus accident on the way home caused by fights, fires, or a distracted bus driver. Hell, I could have just flown out the back of a school bus going down the highway.

I started wrestling and running cross country in middle school, largely to avoid riding the school bus. If you played a sport, you had to stay after school for practice. Yes, I wanted to get into shape and do something besides come home and play video games, but I also hated riding the school bus with everyone else—especially now that I knew that it could mean the end of me. During my final year in middle school, I spent my time after school at one of four places: cross-country practice, wrestling practice, my job, or the library.

Given my build, I didn't think I had a real future as a distance runner, but choosing a sport that felt like a new challenge seemed worthwhile. As for wrestling, I was obsessed with professional wrestling. Instead of staying up until 11:00 p.m. to watch *Monday Night Raw*, I decided to try it myself. I was disappointed when I discovered that wrestling on television was not the same as wrestling in school. Still, I had a lot of fun doing it, and I never would have if I were riding the bus. Wrestling also gave me my first taste of organized combat sports, versus the sporadic brawls I was used to.

The job arose when I got accepted into a program at the Andy Warhol Museum. We made a small magazine that interviewed people from around the city. It paid six dollars an hour for eight hours of work per week. The pay wasn't great, but the job was fun and allowed me to explore some of my interests.

The public library was the final place I used to avoid the torture of the school bus ride home. AMS was a five-minute walk away from the second-largest library in the city. I wasn't there to simply use the internet, though that was part of it. I spent just as much time reading random fantasy novels and checking out books on the Japanese language, astrology, and history. The library was a refuge from more than just the bus rides. It was also the place I went to on weekends. I had no friends in my neighborhood, and I hated being home. Most nights, I stayed at the library until it closed. While a few AMS students showed up after school or on the weekend, none of the kids I fought with in my neighborhood, on the bus, or at school ever went there. It was the first place in my life where I felt safe. I wasn't looking over my shoulder, worrying about whether someone would throw a book or food at me. I didn't have to deal with being called names or fearing for my life. Even today, when I walk past that library, I'm taken back to that feeling of relief and peace.

There was another place where I found relief from the constant stress: the Banksville Gifted Center. The Pittsburgh public school system had a program where students identified as "gifted," first by their teachers and then by an IQ test, were sent to a different school one day a week for more rigorous instruction in writing, math, science, and the humanities. All the schools in the city were assigned to different days of the week, so one day a week, I spent all day with other intelligent kids from different schools.

These were the only kids I had anything in common with. I didn't feel like a particularly smart kid; much of the work at the center frustrated me, and I didn't understand it. But according to the psychologists, I belonged there. I think they were right—but not because of my intelligence.

I just wanted to learn and not be hassled. The standards around me were so low because at my normal school, the teachers were disciplinarians more than educators; they spent more time breaking up fights and dealing with class disruptions than teaching.

I never got into a single fight at the gifted center. No one called me Congo. My stuff never randomly ended up in the toilet. There were never any conflicts on the bus to or from the center, and no one ever opened the back door of the school bus while it was speeding down the highway. It was another place where I could safely be a kid.

The prospect of maintaining that feeling of safety motivated me to apply to Schenley High School. If I didn't go to Schenley, I would have continued to Oliver High School. While it's recently been in the news for shootings, it wasn't the city's worst high school in 1999. It just wasn't the high school I wanted to go to, because all I could see ahead was four more years of the same brutality. Everyone from my neighborhood and AMS would be there. I couldn't imagine enduring four more years of defending myself against frequent physical and psychological abuse.

My mom didn't care what high school I went to—only that I went to one. To her, they were all the same, but I knew better. If you wanted to go to a school different from the one assigned for your neighborhood, you had to get accepted to one of the school's special programs. I researched all the offerings of the schools around the city and decided that Schenley was where I wanted to go, and that I'd get in by applying to their technological vocation program.

The application process was simple. A school with a magnet program admitted a certain number of students each year. Preference went to kids for whom the school was their neighborhood school and those who were continuing from another magnet program. For example, middle school kids taking Spanish, French, Japanese, or German automatically got into Schenley, where those languages were taught at a higher level. After those spots were taken, the remainder were filled by a lottery application system.

The lottery system didn't mean anything if there were fewer applicants than there were spots available. But if there were more, then it was up to chance. I don't know how many applicants there were in 1999, but to give myself the best shot, I badgered my mom and made sure that we were the first in line to apply for Schenley. A few days later, I received a letter telling me I'd gotten in.

III

A New Environment Reveals Old Weaknesses

As the crow flies, Schenley High School was only ten miles away from Northview Heights. By car, along the I-279 highway and I-376 parkway, you could get from my house to Schenley High School in fifteen minutes if there was no traffic. To do so, you had to cross three bridges and a river, but it was a quick trip—if you were a crow, which I was not, or you had a car, which I did not.

I took a public bus to school, as did most kids who lived more than two miles away from the Pittsburgh Public Schools institution they attended. That was the distance you had to reside away from your school to qualify for PPS to cover your transportation. In elementary and middle school, this meant catching a yellow school bus. In high school, we were issued a monthly bus pass. If you lost your bus pass, you had to figure out how to get to school on your own until the next round of bus passes were issued the following month. Taking the city bus meant that I would no longer have to endure or seek refuge from the mayhem of my bus rides in middle school, but this peace came with a trade-off cost: time.

To get to high school, I had to catch two buses. The first was from my neighborhood to downtown, which took twenty-five to thirty minutes. Once downtown, there were a few buses I could take, but they all took another twenty to twenty-five minutes to get to Schenley. After factoring in the five-minute walk to the bus stop, my morning commute to school took about an hour. And that assumed no traffic, detours, weather, or overcrowded buses too full to pick up additional passengers.

Occasionally, the weather would get me into some comically annoying situations. This was in the late '90s and early 2000s, and the internet was nothing like the instantaneous, ubiquitous information disseminator it is today. Cell phones were a rarity, and smartphones weren't invented yet. This meant I found out about weather-related school delays and closings the old-fashioned way: watching them scroll across the bottom of the TV screen during the morning news. Sometimes, the decision to delay or close school was not made until I was already en route. To make matters more annoying, the only reason we ever experienced weather-related delays or closures was due to snow, ice, or extreme cold. So, not only would I make an hour-long trip to a school that was closed, I would be freezing my ass off as I made the trip back home.

A bus being too full to pick me up was a regular occurrence. In the morning, there weren't just thousands of students on their way to school—there were also thousands of adults on their way to work. When the bus was too full, I had to wait for the next bus and, sometimes, the bus after that one. I quickly learned that if I didn't want to spend thirty minutes at the bus stop and arrive late at school anyway, I had to not only leave my house early but also walk farther up the road to another bus stop, earlier in the route, to get on before it got crowded. Again, the trade-off was time.

To guarantee that I got to school on time, I had to leave the house no later than 5:45 a.m. to catch the 6:00 a.m. bus. This meant two things. First, even in the best-case scenario, where I had showered the night before and my clothes were ironed, I had to be awake at 5:30 a.m. I was disciplined and wanted to succeed, as I saw education as my way out of the hellhole of my life, so I made sure that most mornings, the only thing I had to do was wake up and brush my teeth. It also meant that breakfast became a rarely tasted luxury. I didn't have time to eat at home, and there was no way I would make it to free breakfast at school. That started at 6:30 a.m. I was waking up an hour earlier just to make it to the start of the school day at 7:15 a.m.

The other side of this commute was the return trip home. School let out at 2:30 p.m. My high school was located in the Oakland neighborhood of Pittsburgh. Oakland was home to Schenley, Central Catholic, and Oakland Catholic high schools; the University of Pittsburgh; Chatham College; and Carnegie Mellon University. These high schools and universities also had free access to the public transportation system.

Even before we factor in the commuters who weren't students, that's more than fifty thousand people traveling on the bus routes in that part of town. There were a lot of bus routes, but because all the high schools let out at about the same time, they were all packed. So, most days after school, there was a slightly-better-than-zero chance I would get on a bus from Oakland to downtown between 2:30 and 3:30 p.m. During my first year of high school, it was a small miracle if I made it home before 4:30 p.m.

But despite the immense difficulties, I didn't mind. Even with the early mornings and long commute—a commute I usually stood throughout, because the bus was so full—I enjoyed school. More specifically, I enjoyed not being home or around people from my neighborhood.

It's hard to overstate the difference in my life attending Schenley made. I no longer lived with the constant stress of worrying about a fight. Outside of the boxing ring, I haven't been in a fight since I was fourteen. Occasionally, on my commute through downtown Pittsburgh, I'd cross paths with someone I went to middle school with, and they'd get back to calling me Congo, but I was also free of the incessant bullying.

The long commute and school days also meant I was away from home most of the day. Since my mom had started working at a school district even farther away than the school I went to, she didn't bother me too much about not being home. Putting myself in this new environment was the first step toward leaving behind my old life for something better.

Peer Pressure Is Only a Bad Thing
If You Have Bad Peers

Schenley was a melting pot. When discussing diversity, people typically only reference superficial characteristics like race, sex, and nationality. My high school was diverse in this sense of the word, but that was only part of it.

Founded in 1855, Schenley High School was a shining example of fostering diversity. The high school had embraced integration long before the *Brown v. Board of Education* Supreme Court ruling that declared state-sanctioned segregation was unconstitutional. Schenley High School embraced diversity before diversity was cool, and it did it in a way so successful that the school garnered praise from *The New York Times*, the *Los Angeles Times*, and *Newsweek*. In the eighties and nineties, at the height of its academic and social prestige, parents would camp out for days to enroll their children in the alma mater of Andy Warhol, pro wrestler Bruno Sammartino, and saxophonist Stanley Turrentine.

The high school was the only Pittsburgh public school offering the International Baccalaureate (IB) and English as a Second Language (ESL) programs. Four foreign languages were taught. The school graduated nationally ranked math champions and regularly sent students to Ivy League colleges. The IB program attracted top-level students and teachers, the latter being so renowned that parents with the means to send their children to private schools often sent them to Schenley instead.

The school shined not just academically but also in sports and the arts. Schenley was the high school where the Pittsburgh Ballet Theatre sent all of its high school–aged ballerinas. Its champion basketball team regularly sent players to NCAA Division I teams, and the technology program I participated in partnered with Carnegie Mellon University to develop robotics.

During my four years there (1999–2003), the school was 57 percent Black, 13 percent Asian or Latino, and only 30 percent white. Schenley was the feeder school for the Hill District, Bloomfield, Lawrenceville, and Oakland. The Hill District is 97 percent African American, with 40 percent of its residents living below the poverty line, most of them in one of the four housing projects that dominate the area. Lawrenceville and Bloomfield have since been touched by gentrification, but when I was in high school, they were where the poor and lower-class whites in the city lived. At the time, because it was also the only high school that offered ESL classes, many of my classmates were first-generation immigrants.

I lay out Schenley's history and demographics because it's hard to appreciate how different my life and mindset became when I started attending it without understanding my new environment. I knew nothing about the school's demographics or accolades when I applied. I just knew I couldn't continue attending school in my childhood environment.

If you walk the same path as everyone around you, you'll end up at the same destination. However, if your trajectory is just one degree different from everyone else's, you'll eventually be in completely different places.

My earliest deviations from the path of the people around me were, technically speaking, not in my control. PPS picked me for the gifted program; I didn't make that choice. But as soon as I started going to the Banksville center, I saw a world different than the one I'd known my whole life. If not for my weekly visits to the gifted center, I would have never interacted with anyone who lived outside of the hood. While it was only one day a week, this tiny exposure to people from different backgrounds was enough for me to see that there was a different way to live. This motivated me to attend Schenley, where many kids I met at the gifted center were going, rather than the feeder school for my zip code.

My decision to attend a high school on the other side of town, which took one hour and two buses to get to, was a bigger deviation in my life path than the previous one. More importantly, it was my decision, rather than that of the teachers around me. At the time, I didn't fully realize how this decision would affect my approach to the world. In retrospect, though, I recognize that this choice, born out of frustration with my surroundings, became the pivotal point that caused my life to turn out differently than my socioeconomic status might have predicted. Attending a high school in a different part of the city exposed me to new and diverse groups of people, ideas, and opportunities. It broadened my horizons and challenged me to think beyond the limitations of where I was raised. This exposure was crucial in shaping my aspirations and my beliefs about what was possible in my life.

Your Friends Are the Family
You Get to Choose

Once enrolled at Schenley, I found myself alone in this strange world on the other side of town. I didn't know how to connect with anyone. At least when I went to school with other kids from the neighborhood, we all spoke the same language and had similar stories. It wasn't an ideal situation, but it was a community of which I was a part—a community I hated but had a connection with.

I remember asking my new classmates how many fights they'd been in. None of them had ever been in a street fight or fought at school. Here I was, someone who'd been suspended fifteen times for fighting at school and gotten into fights in my neighborhood or on the school bus every other week, and these people had never been in a scuffle.

Most of the time, I just kept to myself, but I eventually made friends. It's impossible to spend eight hours per day with the same people for nine months out of the year and not connect with some of them. During my first year of high school, I met two of my best friends, and it all started over talking trash about who was better at video games.

The only class I had with Eli and Kyle was biology and, initially, I didn't like them. Although our school was diverse, Kyle was one of only three other Black kids in my classes at the time, but he was as different from me as I was from Eli, an upper-middle-class Jewish kid from a predominately Jewish neighborhood.

They were both tall and gangly, over six foot two, and looked like they had never lifted a weight a day in their lives. They always made obscure references to show how much smarter than everyone they were, like knowing the longest word in the dictionary or the scientific name for a camel. They also used to carry around decks of *Magic: The Gathering* cards and consistently caused disruptions because they'd start playing in the middle of class.

Magic: The Gathering is a collectible card game in which players are wizards, casting spells and summoning creatures to battle their opponents. They do this using cards that have different creatures and spells printed on them. This was about as dorky as it sounds and, yeah, these guys were exactly what you imagine when you think "nerd."

Despite our differences, we started bonding over video games— role-playing games, to be precise. *Final Fantasy* and the *Zelda* series were all the rage, and you couldn't be a dork if you didn't play them. I was—as I was learning—closer to being a dork than perhaps I had initially thought.

The other game we all played was *Marvel vs. Capcom*. This incredibly popular fighting game from the 2000s was a crossover of popular Marvel superheroes and characters from the *Street Fighter* series. We'd spend all of our class time talking trash to each other about who was better at the game until we finally decided to settle the debate. After a half-day of school, we all took a forty-minute bus ride to the Monroeville Mall arcade to figure it out once and for all.

I don't remember how many games we played, or the outcome of our initial contest, but after it concluded, Eli's dad picked us up, and we went back to his house for dinner. Since then, we've been great friends, and through Eli and Kyle, I met others who allevi-ated my loneliness. For the most part, I still felt like an outsider, but at least now I had some friends to share class with.

Becoming closer with my new friends and meeting their fami-lies was a great experience, but it was also the first time in my life that I got to see how people outside of the projects lived.

You Don't Know How Bad Things Are Until You Experience Better

Before I went to Schenley, I spent most of my time around people from the hood. Aside from my one day a week at the gifted center, my time was spent in my neighborhood in the projects, or at school with other people from the projects or other low-income, crime-ridden areas.

This meant that for my first fourteen years, I had no concept of a different life. I saw nice families living in the suburbs on televi-sion, but that was just fiction to me. It felt as real to me as the idea of playing in the Super Bowl or being a Hollywood actor. But when I got to Schenley and made new friends, I started to see things dif-ferently. Learning that none of the kids I was around had ever been in a fight before was just the beginning.

The first time I'd ever been in a two-parent household was when I went to Eli's house for dinner after the arcade. All of the friends I made in high school, whether they came from a family with money or they were part of the working class, had a stable environment with both parents involved and caring for them.

They had parents who showed up to support them at their extra-curricular events. Their parents didn't beat them or have anger issues. They had resources, support, and love to help them achieve. I had a mother who got so angry that I wasn't home to do chores that in my senior year she threatened to pull me off the football team, even though she knew that I had a shot at earning a college scholarship by playing.

I want to avoid coming off as ungrateful. Yes, I was a teenager, and teenagers don't always grasp or appreciate the struggles of their parents, but from my perspective, here's how it looked: My mom always had money for cigarettes, weed, and booze, but I had to work all throughout high school so that I'd be able to buy shoes and clothes when I needed them. She had time to bullshit and drink with the neighbors, but not to better herself so we could move out of public housing.

I saw that it didn't have to be this way, and the more I learned from this new life, the more I came to resent my old life. After my ninth-grade year, I did not spend the entirety of a major holiday at home. For Christmas, Thanksgiving, and Easter, I either woke up at a friend's house, stayed the night, or spent the whole day there. And it wasn't just holidays. Most days after school, when I didn't work or have practice, I went to Eli's house, where his family treated me like their own. Even when I had those commitments, I'd go over there afterward instead of heading home.

Eli's family are devoted, observant Jews, and although many of their customs were foreign to me, they embraced me. I was always respectful and curious, so when I had dinner at their home on Fridays, I participated in the Shabbat, reciting the Hebrew prayer before eating. They fed me dinner, and every night, Eli's father drove me home.

They understood the terribleness of my home life, even though I never really talked about it. I give a lot of credit to Eli's dad for driving me home every night, and not just because of the inconvenience. Here was a Jewish man from one of the city's nicest areas who would willingly drive through the projects every night to make sure I got home safely.

Eli's parents weren't the only ones to embrace me in high school. Other friends' parents taught me how to drive, took me to get my license, and stayed with me in the hospital after I had an allergic reaction to tree nuts. Many of them gave me rides home after school. I never minded taking the bus and never expected to be fed, but the support of these caring adults didn't just make my time in high school easier. It showed me another way to live that helped me to leave my previous circumstances behind, physically and mentally.

Being the Best of the Worst
Still Means You're Bad

In addition to revealing how dysfunctional my home life was, high school exposed how little I'd learned in my neighborhood middle school. The constant behavior disruptions had left me woefully unprepared. Sometimes, it was a fight that required security to come to class and escort students out. Other times, it was just kids goofing off to the point where the teacher gave up trying to teach that day's lesson. Occasionally, a teacher would have the energy and motivation to regain control of the class, but this was rare. Most teachers let the students run amok, to maintain their sanity and remain safe.

Those interruptions weren't the only factor that impeded proper learning, though. The curriculum at AMS also lacked academic rigor. The students with the most severe behavioral problems performed the worst academically. Rather than hold struggling students to high standards, teachers made passing easier, so as to avoid failing disruptive students and forcing them to repeat the grade, which would result in another year of having to address their behavioral issues.

In the short term, this approach eased the daily struggle for all parties. The teachers didn't have to force unwilling students to engage, disruptive students didn't have to behave, and no one was left behind. However, in the long term, it failed students who had academic ambition and acuity. Eliminating rigor and complexity sacrificed the educational experience of engaged, promising students.

Entering high school, I had been fooled by the ease of the middle school curriculum into believing I was a strong student. The reality was that I had flourished in a weak system, and nowhere was that clearer than in my understanding of mathematics. It took a lot of work to pass ninth-grade geometry, but I squeaked out a B. This grade primarily resulted from completing all my homework and taking extra credit whenever possible, but the exams demolished me. At the time, I was happy that I passed geometry, but it only set me up for a painful reckoning down the road.

For the rest of high school, I only got Cs and Ds in every math class I took. But grades tell only part of my struggle. Because progression in mathematics depends on securing foundations step-by-step, gaps in my core knowledge inhibited me from digesting new information in later courses. In high school, the quality of the instructors and the class environment were a major improvement on my earlier situation, but lacking the prerequisites, I stalled out before reaching calculus.

Technically speaking, I didn't even graduate high school. In the Pittsburgh public school system, English is the only class you're required to pass all four years to graduate, and in my senior year, I failed. The school gave me a chance to make it up in a condensed version of summer school that took place during the last two weeks of school, but when the teacher discovered I had plagiarized an essay required for that class, he instantly failed me again.

Fortunately, the school administrators still allowed me to walk with my graduation class, and because I had already been accepted to college, the failed English course never impacted my life.

A Stable Home and a Safe Environment Is the Best Thing You Can Give Your Children

When I was younger, I thought poverty was my biggest disadvantage. And while it's true that limited resources narrow your choices, good parents can bridge that gap—especially in a country like the United States, where opportunities are everywhere.

I didn't trust my mom. I didn't want her support or involve-
ment, even if she could give it. My father was in another city and
played no role in my life. I've often wondered which is the worse
fate: to have no relationship with your father or to have a sparse
one with no attempts at guidance or displays of love. My mom always told me I should feel lucky because many kids didn't even
know their father. But what good is knowing him if he plays no
role in your life?

My dad didn't live in the projects, so while he wasn't a high
earner, he wasn't living below the poverty line. Meanwhile, my
mom, sister, and I were, and he did nothing about this. Even if he
felt my mom was unfit to make parenting decisions, he didn't move
closer to us to make a difference in our lives. He'd already shown
my sister and me that our safety and well-being weren't his concern.

Throughout high school, my resentment of my family situation
gradually grew. I couldn't understand how my parents could choose
to have kids and not be prepared to give them the best shot they
could manage. I was angry at my dad for not being a part of my
life and my mom for never trying to improve the quality of it.

In high school, I spent time with many different people of all
races, who had varying levels of family support. All families had
their strengths, weaknesses, flaws, and virtues, but I felt so disad-
vantaged, hustling for money just to take exams or go on school
trips. At the end of the day, this remained the biggest difference
between my peers and me, no matter how much they welcomed
me. I had to make money to support myself, and they didn't—and
this almost ruined all the good momentum I built for myself at
Schenley.

The one friend I had from my neighborhood had a cousin who worked in an adult video store. I worked out a deal where he'd bring videos home. Then I'd record them on VHS tapes and sell them at school. This was in 2002, before the days of free streaming pornography sites. I had a hot product that teenage boys all wanted.

The operation paid for many of the typical activities of my senior year, like my cap and gown and our senior trip, as well as football training equipment. But it eventually got so big that the school administration started investigating me. I was smart enough to stop before they caught me, pocketing nearly two thousand dollars before I had to close up shop. I don't know what would have happened if they had caught me with the tapes, but I know that none of my classmates had to work—let alone sell porn tapes—to take care of themselves and enjoy high school.

Constructive Criticism Can Make Someone's Life Better—Destructive Criticism Always Makes It Worse

When I was a young child, my mom refused to let me play any neighborhood sports. She always told me that she didn't want people to see me as just another Black boy from the projects who was only good at sports. Before I got to high school, I didn't mind, because it kept me away from the neighborhood kids—not to mention that I was terrible at basketball. Perhaps I could have developed some skills with practice, but no one was interested in teaching me, and I didn't want to be around the people in my neighborhood anyway.

High school gym class was the first time I discovered that I had any athletic ability. In class, we had to take a series of physical ability tests: push-ups, max bench press, swimming, a timed one-mile run around the school, standing broad jump, and the forty-yard dash. Now, you didn't need to do rock-star numbers to pass, but if you could place on the leaderboard, then you'd get extra credit. Plus, the bragging rights and admiration weren't bad either.

In the ninth grade, I discovered that I could bench press 225 pounds and run the forty-yard dash in 4.7 seconds. At that point, all the guys in my gym class who played football wanted me to join the team, although I had never played the game and knew nothing about it. I had never even watched an entire football game, but it seemed like something to try. I was looking for any reason not to be at home or in my neighborhood. Summer and after-school practices gave me an excuse to stay out of both. I also wanted to feel special and stand out in some way.

I never felt like people liked me simply for who I was. I always believed that if I didn't have a special talent or skill or stand out somehow, people wouldn't want anything to do with me. This mindset resulted from constantly fighting at school, being neglected by my father, and feeling like my mom didn't approve of me because I was "just like my father." When I combined those experiences with being in another school where I was so different and isolated, the chip on my shoulder only got heavier.

The good thing about this type of inferiority complex is that it drives you to push yourself and accomplish more. I joined the football team partly because I wanted to compete but also because I wanted to belong.

I started playing football during my sophomore year of high school. In my first year playing, I was put on the junior varsity team. Our high school was coming off an undefeated season that saw Schenley capture the City League championship, with many players returning for the new year. Despite being bigger and faster than many others, I knew nothing about the game, but I enjoyed practicing and learning.

Although I was improving, I wasn't good enough to be a varsity player, even on the second string. And since this was my first time in an organized sporting environment with teammates, there were certain parts of the etiquette that I didn't understand. This revealed itself in the final game of the season.

The junior varsity season ended two games before the regular varsity season, and I had hated my experience at the first of those games, sitting on the sidelines—not even dressed, just standing there doing nothing. I figured I wouldn't be missed, and I decided not to travel with the rest of the team for the second game and to watch it as a spectator instead. But Coach Trent had another idea entirely. He spotted me before the game and pulled me aside.

"Why aren't you down here with the team?" His tone was serious, but not threatening.

"The JV season is over, and I'm not even suited up, so there's no way I'm gonna get put in the game. So, I ain't think you'd miss me. Not like there's anything for me to do."

There are moments when you have an opportunity to teach or

punish, and your decisions will have an impact on the rest of a person's life. No one would have been surprised if the coach loudly chewed me out, kicked me off the team, and banned me from ever playing at Schenley High School again. He didn't do any of that.

"I got you. I know it sucks, but you're part of the team, and that means doing what the team does. Everyone on the field today paid their dues, and you gotta do the same."

He could sense my distress at busting my ass, getting better, and being forced to travel when I wasn't suiting up. Before I could open my mouth to agree, he continued.

"Now, I can't make you do anything but follow the rules to be part of this team. You can either join us on the sidelines or don't bother playing for me next season."

I'm happy that Coach Trent approached me as if I didn't know the rules rather than assuming I was outright breaking them. This interaction was a perfect example of constructive criticism, a form of negative feedback that is essential for growth and development. He pointed out where I had misunderstood how a team worked and provided me with an opportunity to correct my behavior.

Coach Trent's feedback was specific and focused on what I did wrong, but it also gave me a clear path to make it right. He didn't attack my character or make me feel like a failure. Instead, he offered guidance on how to improve and be a better teammate. If Coach Trent had berated me, kicked me off the team, and banned me from playing in the future, that would have been destructive criticism. It would have focused on my shortcomings without providing any direction for improvement, likely crushing my confidence and my desire to continue with football.

Constructive criticism, like the feedback I received from Coach Trent, is vital for identifying weaknesses and learning from mistakes. However, receiving positive feedback when you've made progress or achieved success is equally important. If Coach had only pointed out my flaws, without acknowledging my efforts and improvements, I might have become discouraged and lost motivation.

The right balance of constructive criticism and positive reinforcement is key to personal growth and development. Too much of either can be detrimental, leading to a sense of defeat or an inflated ego. Coach Trent seemed to understand this, using the opportunity to teach me a valuable lesson while still leaving the door open for me to continue playing football and improving as a teammate. His constructive criticism taught me the value of commitment and being part of something greater than myself. The lesson went beyond football, shaping my approach to life by instilling the importance of perseverance, teamwork, and learning from mistakes. It allowed me to embrace the positive changes in my life instead of slipping back into an environment that would have held me down.

Life will keep giving you the same test until you pass it. And even then, it likes to occasionally give you a pop quiz to make sure you didn't forget. When I got to college, in the summer of 2003, life tested me to see if I had retained Coach Trent's lesson, and I failed badly.

But in high school, for the first time, football gave me a clear goal for what to do with my life—even if that goal wasn't necessarily realistic or likely. I wouldn't understand how beneficial that goal had been until after it was gone.

IV

If You Ain't Got a Dream, You Ain't Got Nothin'

When I started playing football, everyone thought I'd make an excellent inside linebacker. I was big, strong, and quick, but athletic skills are only part of what you need to be a successful linebacker. You need instincts, and those instincts come from watching and playing a lot of games. Since my mom never let me play sports growing up, and we didn't watch them at home, I knew nothing about football and had zero instincts.

Linebackers have been called "the quarterbacks of the defense." I had Division I–level athleticism, but I had only been playing for one year when I became a starter in high school. I was terrible at the position. I blossomed into an all-city player when they switched me to defensive end, a more raw and instinctual position.

I loved the game and wanted to play at the highest level. That meant getting into a Division I school with a big football program. Collegiate football (and collegiate sports) are divided by the NCAA into Divisions I, II, and III. Most professional players come from the Division I level, because those schools have the money to offer scholarships and seriously invest in player development. As a result, Division I schools can easily recruit the best players.

However, Georgetown University was the only Division I school that showed interest in me, and my low grades and SAT scores caused them to revoke the offer. I still wanted to play football at a high level, so I didn't let this deter my dreams. I learned that there was another way.

After receiving no interest from Division I schools and losing my only offer, my new plan was to "walk on" to the University of Pittsburgh football team. Walk-ons are players who weren't offered a scholarship, so they try out. If they prove they have what it takes, they make the team and are given a scholarship. While I didn't start playing football until my sophomore year of high school and was shorter than average for defensive ends, I figured that with hard work, I might have a chance at making football more than a hobby for me.

While I didn't know what to do with my life when I graduated from college, I knew what I *didn't* want. I didn't want to be broke, and I knew—or at least believed—that I was either bad at or had no interest in the subjects that guaranteed a decent prospect of employment. I also didn't want to have a boring life. I'd achieve all those goals if I could get to the NFL, or even the Canadian Football League. I could make a little money, not be bored, and do something interesting. A boy can dream, right?

In 2016, the NCAA reported there were 1,083,308 high school football players, with 73,660 (about 6.8 percent) of them going on to play in college. Of these, only 22 percent (16,205), mostly seniors, were NFL draft–eligible. However, with just 252 NFL draft spots available that year, only 1 in 64 eligible players made it to the pros.

Players don't have to be drafted: They can also make the NFL through free agency or by being called up from lesser leagues, like the CFL. Regardless, my chances of getting into the NFL were grim. The odds of a high school player making it to the NFL are about 0.023 percent. To put that number in perspective, your odds of getting struck by lightning at some point are 0.006 percent. You're only four times more likely to make it to the NFL than to be hit by a bolt of electricity from the sky.

I knew the odds were long, but I figured I might as well give it a shot. This decision paid off, but not in the way that I expected it would: By committing to the pursuit of my dream, I unwittingly gave myself a goal that I could rally around, something that could organize my life and give me clarity and focus that went beyond the football field.

But at the time, I genuinely believed I could be one of the lucky few to make it to the NFL. I obsessively tracked stats and idolized players who defied the odds—those who started late, were undersized, or came from small schools. London Fletcher, a linebacker from Division III John Carroll University, had a Hall of Fame–worthy career despite going undrafted. Santana Moss, a walk-on at the University of Miami, broke records and had an outstanding NFL career. These stories fueled my determination, proving that no matter how unlikely, the path to the NFL was possible. When chasing a dream, you need that proof to keep believing.

I studied the metrics of every player drafted, comparing myself to them and setting goals for my physical ability. By the end of my high school football career, I weighed 250 pounds, could bench press 345 pounds, and ran a 4.55-second forty-yard dash. These were numbers that matched up well with players who made it to the league. The next step would be to find a college, preferably in Division I, where I could walk onto the team and prove myself at the highest level.

My plan hit a snag when the University of Rochester, a small Division III school, showed interest in me. My goal was the NFL, and I saw myself as an underdog battling against long odds. I had no intention of making that journey any harder than it had to be. Walking on at a Division I school like the University of Pittsburgh might be a long shot, but it seemed the best route to success. And so, at first, I dismissed the idea of attending Rochester.

However, when the parents of my upper-middle-class friends learned about the opportunity, they insisted I'd be foolish to pass it up. With two of my friends' parents having attended the school, their repeated encouragement made me reconsider and, gradually, the prospect of a prestigious degree started to look more and more appealing. The chance of escaping poverty with a degree from

Rochester seemed more realistic than the slim odds of making it to the NFL. Opting for a more secure future over a risky dream began to make sense—at least, that's what I hoped.

I arrived at the University of Rochester in August of 2003, and I quickly found out that I didn't like football nearly as much when it demanded so much time. While it seems obvious that collegiate football would require a large investment of time, I had not fully considered how much of my life would revolve around it and, at the Division III level, how scant the rewards were for that investment.

For starters, there was no scholarship money. Division III schools don't give any aid based on athletic ability. While, at the time, no collegiate athlete at any level received direct monetary compensation—this has changed due to the recently revised NCAA rules that now permit student athletes to profit from their name, image, and likeness, opening the door to sponsorship deals—at the Division I level, free tuition and housing were at least compensation for the hours of work. While the NCAA mandates that "student-athlete participation in countable athletically related activities shall be limited to a maximum of four hours per day and twenty hours per week," that time doesn't include dressing, showering, and taping before the athletic event.

Between workouts, film study, and games (some of which included travel), I dedicated between thirty and thirty-five hours a week to football. Since I was attending the school on a financial aid package that included federal student loans, it was the worst of both worlds: I wasn't truly receiving a free education, but my time investment was that of an athlete who was.

On top of that, I had no clear goals outside of football. I entered college with no idea of what I wanted to study. I just knew what I wanted to avoid—math or anything quantitative. My high school experience with math demolished any confidence I had that I could handle the subject.

But at the same time, I knew that most non-STEM majors would hurt my future earning potential. Plus, non-STEM subjects seemed more about arguing for the right answer, which didn't appeal to me. This ruled out majors like English, philosophy, and sociology. The only path that seemed both exciting and feasible was learning a foreign language. In a time before the current abundance of online language-learning resources, this felt like a smart investment and a cool skill to have.

As a freshman juggling financial aid and football, I had to manage both a full course load and a full-time athletic commitment. Alongside mandatory biology and math classes, I filled my schedule with foreign languages. Since I had excelled in Japanese in high school, I chose Japanese 101 and Spanish 101 to balance the load and play to my strengths. To round it out, I also took a class on programming the old HTML language.

My first semester should have been a breeze, but I discovered something else: I had no business being in college, and not just because of the academics. As soon as my environment changed, my dream would be severely tested.

No Guidance Is Just as Destructive as Bad Guidance

I wasn't prepared for the level of autonomy granted to a college student. I figured handling the work would be easy, because I lived right on campus and no longer had to spend two hours commuting to and from school each day. I also thought that because my mom wasn't involved in my middle and high school academic life, and I had still managed to graduate, I'd be fine in the relatively lawless collegiate environment. However, my life quickly fell apart.

In the Greek epic poem *The Odyssey*, Odysseus is sailing his men home after the Trojan War, and he's warned by the gods about the deadly Sirens—monsters that assume the form of beautiful women and use their enchanting voices to lure sailors to their doom. To defend his crew from falling victim to the Sirens' charms, Odysseus orders everyone to stuff their ears with beeswax. But he's curious—can these girls really pump vocals like that, or is it just a hype job? To find out, he instructs his men to tie him to the ship's mast and remove the beeswax.

Turns out, the hype was real! The Sirens could really belt it out. Odysseus wanted so badly to join their party that he tried to break free from the ropes, cutting his arms in the process. Thankfully, his crew kept him restrained, saving them all from disaster.

My closest friends in high school all came from loving and stable families. Their parents were the type of parents who were invested in their children's lives and the lives of their children's friends. They treated me, at worst, as their child's best friend. At best, the only way you knew I wasn't one of their own was because of our racial differences.

So while I lacked a stable and supportive home life, I had the next best thing: I had friends who lived in stable and supportive homes with families who welcomed me as if I were their own. While they had no technical authority over me to make me do my homework, the influence of being around their disciplined children was more than enough. In my high school odyssey, they were the crew that tied me to the mast and stuffed beeswax in my ears.

Going to college was my release from all the restraints. As soon as I was on my own, I crashed headfirst into heavy drinking, partying, and chasing girls. I no longer had the positive influence of my friends and their families, so my negative traits took over. I couldn't resist the Sirens' call.

I spent my days working out and playing football and my free time chasing girls, playing video games, and blowing a windfall of life insurance money I had gotten from my dad's death earlier that year on dumb shit like video games I'd never play, anime I'd never watch, and food I didn't need because of the college meal plan I was on. I also drank—a lot.

Unlike most college freshmen, I hadn't had so much as a sip of alcohol in my youth. Despite living with an alcoholic mother who always had beer and liquor in the house, I was terrified of getting my ass kicked by her for drinking. On top of that, I hated how my mom acted when she drank, and I hated how my mom always had the money for booze, cigarettes, and marijuana, yet we lived in the projects and relied on food banks and public assistance. The whole mentality seemed backward, and I wanted nothing to do with it.

In high school, where people typically start their relationship with alcohol, I also did not drink. None of my friends drank, so neither did I. I liked my friends, and we thought we were cool, but none of them were the type to go to or throw crazy parties, where teenage drinking typically occurs.

I didn't have my first drink until I was eighteen, on a visit to the University of Rochester. It was cheap Miller Lite from a keg in a frat party basement. I remember thinking this must be what old boots taste like after a five-mile trek through the snow has chilled the foot sweat. The first red plastic cup of this cheap swill tasted terrible, as did the second, but by the third cup, I'd found true love. Truth be told, getting drunk and making out with girls in a musty basement with beer-stained floors had just as big an influence on my decision to go to Rochester as my friends' parents did.

When I arrived at college, I learned that as long as you only drank on Thursday, Friday, Saturday, or a night when you didn't have class the next day, you were OK. As long as you only drank on those days, from dusk till dawn, you didn't have a problem. As long as you didn't break the law or end up in the hospital, no one questioned your drinking habits.

It was like the premise of the horror movie *The Purge*, except instead of all crime being legal for twenty-four hours, all levels of intoxication were acceptable during those days—as long as it didn't bleed into the daytime hours. I followed those rules for two semesters, but while I might have thought this was controlled chaos, it turned out it was pure pandemonium.

Because of this exhausting lifestyle, I rarely made it to class. That first semester, my best grade was a C, in Japanese 101. It wasn't for lack of strong performance on tests and quizzes, but a large part of my grade was based on attendance and homework. I hardly showed up, and I never did homework. My GPA in the first semester of college was 1.2, the lowest on the football team by far. I was put on academic probation, which motivated me to do only slightly better the next semester. I improved my GPA to a 2.1, barely good enough to stay enrolled.

During the third semester, I hardly went to class. Unlike my first year at the University of Rochester, my absence from class in my sophomore year wasn't motivated by partying and drinking. I missed the deadline to secure housing on campus, but I wasn't allowed to live off campus, so I got relegated to a stretch of university-owned apartments reserved for grad students, a mile off campus. I'm not lazy and was in shape, but I hated walking to and from campus every day.

By now, the reality of my chances to make it to the NFL, the CFL, or any of the developmental leagues had set in. Nothing had changed about the odds. Those were still nearly zero, but I had grown more aware of my limitations. I was too short, too slow, and my skills weren't developing quickly enough. Worse, I was quickly losing interest in football—the only thing that had been motivating me to keep trying at college.

A Fixed Mindset Is the Fastest Way to Failure

As defined by psychologist Carol Dweck, a "fixed mindset" is the belief that one's abilities, intelligence, and talents are inherent, static traits that cannot be significantly changed or improved through effort and practice. People with a fixed mindset often believe that they are either naturally gifted at something or they are not, and that there is little they can do to change that.

The opposite of this is a "growth mindset." People with a growth mindset view their abilities, intelligence, and talent as malleable. If you believe that talent and luck make one person better than another, then you're afflicted with a fixed mindset. If you think that practice can grow your abilities and that, given enough time, you can learn or improve on anything, then you're blessed with a growth mindset.

It doesn't matter which mindset is a more accurate representation of reality. The only thing that matters is which one you *believe* to be true, because that belief will affect your approach to life's challenges.

You won't attempt to change something if you don't believe you can. Whenever you hear someone say they "aren't a math person," they're operating under the belief that mathematical ability is an intrinsic, immutable trait. Rather than trying to improve their weakness, this type of person will assume they can do nothing and accept their limitation. A fixed mindset robs a person of grit and resilience, two essential skills for success in any domain, because everything worthwhile will, at some point, challenge you.

When the school system labeled me as gifted, it gave me a chance to meet people from beyond my circumstances. Those interactions and experiences motivated me to attend a different high school in a different environment. Seeing that there was another way to live, I was hopeful about what I could achieve. The counterintuitive downside of the label is that it made me believe I was a smart kid and that my ability to learn was high, but fixed. As a result, I interpreted any academic, athletic, or personal shortcoming as a predestined genetic deficiency that I could do nothing about.

The same fixed mindset that had made me avoid math because I figured there was no way I could improve was now manifesting itself in football. Although my first semester of college was an academic disaster, I had earned the starting defensive end position when I got to campus. However, after a few terrible outings, I lost that job halfway through the first season and was on the bench for the entire first game of the second season. Once I was no longer treated like a standout with talent and had been relegated to second-string status, I figured there was no point to playing. So, after the first game of my second season, I quit the team.

I was tested on the lesson my high school football coach taught me, and I failed.

By August 2004, the start of my third semester at the University of Rochester, I also had another problem: money. My bank account was overdrawn by three hundred dollars. I also had student-loan debt, but I didn't consider that real money, since I never touched it and it only went toward university expenses. I think most nineteen-year-olds—especially those who grew up poor and had no role models to teach them about money—look at student loans this way. They know it's money, but they can't understand where it came from or what paying it back looks like.

What made this situation even worse is that I'd recently received a windfall that should've helped stabilize me at college. My father had died in May 2003, leaving me with $55,000 in life insurance money. To this day, I still can't remember anything I bought from all that money—only the bad decisions I made with it. For example, I picked up the payments for his 2001 Chrysler Sebring, believing that the car simply passed to me as his only son and rightful heir.

Well, it turns out that when someone dies with an outstanding car loan, the loan isn't automatically transferrable. I had to either pay it off completely or turn in the car. I didn't learn this until after I'd paid the car note for over a year, and then they came and repossessed it anyway. The bank gave me an option: I could turn in the car or have a warrant issued for my arrest. I gave up the car because, by that time, I had already spent every dollar—and then some—of the $55K.

One of the kids on the football team and his family happened to be from Pittsburgh, and they were kind enough to pick me up and drive me to campus that year. The Sunday before they picked me up, I went to the bank and withdrew as much money as I could. I managed to get about four hundred dollars—about three hundred dollars more than I actually had—before the ATM stopped letting me take money out. I stretched that four hundred dollars as far as possible, but eventually, I was stuck in Rochester, New York, without a dime to my name.

At this point, the choice was simple: I was failing all of my classes, had been effectively removed from campus social life, had quit playing football, and hated being at college. So, before they could fire me, I quit. Giving up on my football dream had led, in no time at all, to the collapse of my whole life. But this still left me with a major problem: What would I do once the university realized I was no longer a student and kicked me out of my apartment?

I'd Rather Be Broke Together
Than Rich Alone

Among the many reasons to be kind to people is that you never know when you'll need to rely on the kindness of others. This doesn't mean you're only helpful because you expect others to help you. That approach will set you up for bitterness and disappointment. Karma is a sloppy art that doesn't always get it right, but you gain nothing by not helping when it would be easy for you.

You should be kind because it genuinely makes you feel better and makes the world a better place to live. However, when karma does get things right, and you desperately need assistance, it's amazing how it can turn a bad situation into something good or take a good situation and make it something great.

One of the reasons for my struggles at the University of Rochester was that I had trouble finding friends. I wasn't an antisocial guy: I was overly social. Between playing football, the chess club, anime movie nights, partying, and dating, I was rarely alone. However, this emphasis on quantity left no room for quality.

I don't mean that I wasn't meeting quality people. But I had trouble connecting with people beyond the superficial circumstances that initially brought us together. I had people to drink with, people to play video games with, and people to play chess with, but I didn't feel like I knew anyone outside of these environments. I had people to do stuff with, but I didn't make many friends because of my fear that people only liked what I *did* rather than who I *was*.

This fear was exacerbated by my socioeconomic status on campus relative to the other students. No one else on campus was poor, Black, raised by a single mother, and from the inner-city projects. While none of my close friends back home fit this demographic either, they had an innate understanding of it because they spent so much time around me, and many of them knew plenty of other people in similar situations. However, some Black kids at Rochester didn't even believe I grew up in the projects. While this was meant as a compliment, it also showed that just because someone is the same race as you doesn't mean they have the same experiences, perspectives, or opinions.

I did become close friends with one guy, Jay Leuthe. We didn't party together that often, but we played a lot of video games, had a lot of chats about things outside of football, and had had a similar path in life growing up. He was a local kid from the inner city of Rochester.

During my second semester there, I had the car I thought I'd inherited on campus with me, and Jay often asked me to use it to run errands or take girls out on dates. A few times I let him borrow it for the entire weekend. I drove home a lot, as it was only a four-hour drive between Rochester and Pittsburgh, but I let him use it whenever I was on campus. There was never any problem, and I never expected anything from him. He was my friend; we had laughs and we had arguments. He was one of only three guys with whom I built a genuine connection.

Well, after I submitted my withdrawal from the school, I told him all about it.

"So what are you gonna do now?" he asked over lunch one day in the quad.

"Scraping up some money for a Greyhound bus ticket back to Pittsburgh. Shit, that's all I can do. Imma stay with my aunt."

Jay went silent for a moment, almost as if I had said something wrong.

"What?"

"Look. I got a car now, and I'm driving down to Philly this weekend to visit my girl. If you want, I could give you a ride on the way there."

If you don't know the mid-Atlantic region, Pittsburgh is *not* on the way from Rochester, New York, to Philadelphia. Pittsburgh and Philadelphia are at opposite ends of Pennsylvania. No route from Rochester puts those places on the way to and from each other. I believe that Jay would have been much better at geography if I hadn't been so generous to him the previous year by letting him use my car.

Once I was back home, it was fun to see my girlfriend and my old friends, but I found myself in a rough position. I was effectively homeless. When I later wrote about this point in my life in a newsletter, my mom got angry enough to tell me that it was my choice and I could have come home. While that was technically true, living with my mom wasn't really an option for me. I spent hardly any time there in high school because we had such a tumultuous relationship. I wish that we had the type of connection where I wouldn't have hesitated to move back in, but too many things about my mom and her life made me too angry to even consider it.

Fortunately, my aunt took me in. She lived in a small two-bedroom apartment with three adult children and their grandchildren. I slept on the floor where her son usually slept, except for the nights he worked. It wasn't comfortable, but it kept me from actually being homeless. On the nights he didn't work, I *still* slept on the floor—just not in the comfy nook behind the couch.

I had three challenges right off the bat: I didn't have a job, food, or transportation. Solving the transportation issue was illegal but simple: I made photocopies of the bus passes that my friends still in high school had, or I made a bootleg copy of my friend Kyle's ID from Carnegie Mellon University, so I could ride the bus.

Food was a little trickier and still required a bit of lawbreaking. I'd steal a pack of Pringles and a bottle of soda from a Rite Aid I had scouted. I knew where all the security cameras were and the best times to shoplift. I eventually learned that most places don't care if you shoplift. You don't attract attention as long as you aren't blatantly walking out of the store with stuff you never paid for. I was 255 pounds of muscle, much bigger than any security guard. Even if they caught me, they didn't want to try to stop me over four dollars in junk food.

I eventually got a job at the video game retailer GameStop. I thought this job would be a dream because I loved playing video games, but it turns out that playing and selling them are two completely different things. I didn't hate the job, but I didn't like it either. It was minimum-wage customer service, where I was expected to make insurance upsells on each purchase, even though no bonus or incentive was given for success other than that I wouldn't get fired. At least I liked the people I worked with, and I saved up enough to rent an apartment with two other friends. We got lucky and found an apartment willing to rent to three twenty-year-old guys with part-time jobs. The apartment was in a decent neighborhood and nicer than the $550 rent would make it seem. We didn't have any furniture, our beds were on the floor, and my room was just a converted living room, but we made it work and had more fun than our bank accounts would suggest was possible.

I always tell young adults that some of their happiest moments will be living with a few roommates in a place barely fit for crackheads, surviving off canned tuna and ramen noodles. Once you make it past that point, you'll never want to go back, but hopefully, during this phase of your life, you'll learn that money does not buy happiness. Only solid relationships and good experiences accomplish this, and one of the best—albeit hardest—ways to learn this lesson is by living in poverty with your closest friends.

Rapper Jadakiss said it best in the song "Show Discipline": "I'd rather be broke together than rich alone." The problem was that I could only live this way for so long before the absence of a sustaining goal caught up to me. At first, I tried to ignore this fact, but soon it was made painfully clear.

If the Truth Hurts, You Probably Needed to Hear It

After three semesters of academic probation, failing grades, and multiple citations for drinking, the University of Rochester had finally had enough—they were kicking me out. I had no delusions about my performance at the school, so before they could force me out, I "voluntarily withdrew." I basically said to them, "You can't fire me! I quit!"

But when I left, I took two things with me: an alcohol problem and a disdain for the higher education system. So I spent the next two years of my life working minimum-wage, dead-end jobs to finance my drinking, all while entertaining the fantasy that I had more in common with Steve Jobs or Larry Ellison—famous college dropouts who became billionaires—than I did with the homeless guys I'd pay to buy liquor for me since I was underage.

I'd tell anyone who would listen how pointless college was and how you could do anything without a college degree. Dr. Laurel Roberts was one of the people who had to endure my rants and criticisms against college. Because she was my girlfriend's mother and I spent most of my time with my girlfriend, she heard all about how college was an overpriced scam and how many successful people there are who haven't gone to college.

My rants annoyed her for multiple reasons. First, she was a biology professor at the University of Pittsburgh. Second, it's not like I was an example of one of those successful people who made it without going to college. I was a college dropout working at Starbucks, where I'd gone to work after losing my job at GameStop because they didn't need the extra help anymore.

On top of that, she was technically funding my life. I ate all of my meals at her house, had a key to let myself in for lunch if no one was home, and only had a cell phone because I was on her family phone plan. One day, she finally lost her patience as I went through one of my rants, and she hit me with the question that finally forced me to take a long, hard look at myself: *"So, let's say that you're right—that college is worthless—well, what have you done with your life in the past four years besides show up at my house every day and eat my food?"*

After with that, she threw me out. It was December 2006, and Professor Roberts had finally run out of patience. She refused to continue entertaining the criticisms of a twenty-two-year-old alcoholic, college-dropout, minimum-wage-earning Starbucks barista. Dr. Roberts had tolerated me in the past for the sake of my relationship with her daughter. But on that day, she'd finally had enough.

It was the most humiliating thing I'd ever experienced up to that point in my life. I wasn't angry because my pride had been wounded. I wasn't sad because my ego had been shattered. I was holding back tears and stumbling over words that never escaped my mouth because she brought attention to the deficiencies and insecurities that I had been ignoring for so long. The blood boiling in my face and dryness in my throat told me she was right—I had made no progress since high school. In truth, I had regressed.

It was like the tale of the fox and the sour grapes. In that fable, a fox sees a bunch of grapes hanging from a vine and tries to reach them, but they are too high. After several failed attempts, the fox gives up and walks away, dismissively claiming that the grapes were probably sour anyway. The moral of the story is that people often disparage what they cannot have to make themselves feel better about not having it.

I was the fox, and college was my bunch of grapes. I had convinced myself that higher education was worthless because I failed to succeed at it. It was easier to criticize the system than to confront my shortcomings and take responsibility for my actions. By dismissing the value of college, I attempted to minimize the dissonance between my desires and reality. But just like the fox dismissing the grapes, my criticism of college was a flimsy excuse. Dr. Roberts saw right through it and called me out on my lack of progress and direction.

Her words stung because they were true. I had been deluding myself, trying to protect my ego from the painful reality of my situation: I shared a furnitureless apartment with friends, and most months, I could only afford two out of the following three living expenses: rent, bills, or groceries. My job at Starbucks paid me $7.25 per hour, which couldn't cover everything, even working forty hours a week. How did I survive? Because of Dr. Roberts. As she so bluntly pointed out, I spent every day at her house, eating her food, and thanks to that food—and my increasingly self-destructive relationship with alcohol—I had ballooned to more than 280 pounds since quitting football.

Dr. Roberts calling me out on my bullshit was the catalyst for a massive change. As embarrassing as it was, that brief, painful exchange was necessary. Now, I knew that I needed to do something—I needed a new dream that could replace my old one of playing pro football. I just wasn't sure exactly what it could be. After barely graduating high school and failing out of college, I lacked faith in my cognitive abilities. Even if I did muster the confidence, I was barely making enough money to survive by working full-time. I could not afford to stop working to attend school, but I also lacked the connections and skills to embark on a more promising career path if I didn't finish my education. And even if I did find a better job, I would need a car—I couldn't get by on my counterfeit bus passes forever.

What were my options? I needed a steady source of income to pay my bills, so working in commission-based sales was also out of the question. The last option I looked at was the military, but this was during the Iraq War, and as badly as I wanted to change my life, I didn't want to take a bullet in the desert. And I didn't want to leave the familiarity of everything I knew.

So there I was, without any reasonable prospects for improving my earning capacity—but the problem was about more than that. My lack of a high-paying job wasn't the focal point of Dr. Roberts's rebuke. She hadn't mentioned money or career at all. *"What have you done with your life in the past four years besides show up at my house every day and eat my food?"*

This question was a matter of sweat equity and personal development. I had nothing to show that I had applied myself to anything. I couldn't play an instrument or speak another language. I hadn't put time into any causes or built anything enduring. I didn't have any talents, skills, or abilities. I didn't even have the health to show that I had stuck to a disciplined diet and training regimen.

With all this in mind, I decided to change my focus. I set out to find something to invest myself in that would generate a positive return on my character: a new dream. I started—as the Most Interesting Man in the World used to say in those Dos Equis commercials that ran in the 2000s—to "beef up my obituary."

Around this same time, YouTube launched, and once I discovered it, I spent most of my free time on that platform, watching music videos and professional fights of all disciplines. Kickboxing, MMA, vale tudo—it didn't matter what it was, as long as it involved two men beating the heck out of each other. When I started considering what I might apply myself to, I realized that maybe I could be one of those men. Unlike most other sports in the United States, you don't have to be enrolled in college to compete in combat sports, and there is no age limit on when you can start competing.

I didn't know if I'd be any good at boxing, but I knew the only way to discover my potential was to try. After watching hours of fighters going at it, I knew one thing for certain: I had the pain tolerance to fight. I'd been in street fights before, and from my days as a football player, I knew about the dedication and intensity required to train for a sport. At this point in my boxing journey, I didn't know much about the requirements of a fighter beyond the fact that he needed to work hard and be able to take punches as well as he gave them. I had those two traits going for me, plus a third, even more important asset: I didn't have anything to lose.

In the worst-case scenario, I'd be terrible at boxing. I'd get beat up and embarrassed to the point where I'd have to quit. I'd tell everyone I used to be a fighter, like guys in their thirties who still talk about being standout athletes in high school. At the very least, even while losing, I'd have some cool stories to help me pick up girls at the bar. In other words, my life wouldn't change much, but I could say I tried something that many people are terrified of.

In the best-case scenario, who knew what could happen? Maybe I could make the Olympic team or become locally famous. Top boxers who headlined events made millions and were celebrities. Even if I never made it that far, I figured I'd at least reach a point where I'd make enough money to pay my rent. Either way, I made up my mind: At twenty-two years old, I'd take up boxing.

I had a new dream. Now I just had to find a gym that I could get to on the bus, because I still couldn't afford a car.

V

Make Things Happen, or Things Happen to You

n the 2002 boxing drama *Undisputed*, George "Iceman" Chambers remarks, "People play baseball. Nobody plays boxing. I'm not an athlete. I'm a gladiator."

As a boxer, you aren't just playing a game—you're risking your life. Fighters waive their right to sue for injuries sustained within the bout's rules. You might not be trying to *literally* kill your opponent, but there is always the chance that this might actually happen. According to the Marquess of Queensberry rules—modern boxing's foundation—striking a standing man to death is actually legal.

That means that there's a contradiction at the heart of boxing—a contradiction between what you've been told to do all your life, and what you're trying to do now. I once witnessed two boxing clubs nearly brawl during sparring until a coach intervened, shouting: "Do this on the street and they'll put you in jail. Do it in the ring and they'll cheer and pay your bills!"

Nothing else in life sanctions physical violence. Other sports prohibit fighting, with varying penalties. MMA and boxing not only allow it but use it to keep score and determine victory.

To succeed in boxing, you must hone your ability to deliver and withstand physical punishment if you have any hope of surviving, much less succeeding. This demands seriously training your body, mind, and heart. When I started boxing, I had just spent the last four years since quitting football screwing around and not applying myself to anything. I quickly learned not just the value of working hard but the value of working smart.

Just Because You Can Punch Doesn't Mean You Can Fight

When I started my amateur boxing journey, in 2008, I won more due to raw aggression and dumb luck than athleticism or skill. The grainy footage of my first fight demonstrates how terrible my boxing was. Both my opponent and I were swinging for the fences, but my left hook happened to connect first, and down he went. It looked more like a street fight between thugs than a sanctioned bout between athletes.

"So, what's your plan for when you face someone you just can't knock out?" Matt asked, sipping on a Long Island iced tea after my first victory. He was one of the friends I'd made when I started at Schenley High School and was also one of my main drinking buddies.

"I'll figure it out," I said, shrugging off the question. "In the meantime, let's drink!"

I never learned the proper ingredients for a Long Island. All I knew was that it was strong enough to quickly get you drunk without tasting the corrosive tang of whatever 100-proof mixture you were ingesting.

I thought Matt's question was annoying. I had just won my first fight, and here this guy was asking me what I was gonna do if I couldn't win. But the truth was that it was a fair question, and it was one that I'd eventually have to find the answer to if I wanted to have a real shot.

During those first three years of my boxing career, I made marginal improvements between each fight. But I wasn't learning the sweet science of hitting and not getting hit. I wasn't learning how to *box*. I was beating the crap out of guys, but when they figured out how to avoid my power punches—which I threw with inferior technique—I lost.

From January 2008 to March 2011, my record was 13–5, with all thirteen wins by knockout. Although this record and the knockout wins may initially seem impressive, upon deeper analysis, those wins demonstrate more my weaknesses rather than my strengths.

Eighteen fights in three years is a snail's pace. To put this in perspective, my friend Cam F. Awesome, the most decorated amateur heavyweight in the United States, had almost a hundred fights in his first three years of competing. If you look up any of

Cam's fights on YouTube, you'll see that he doesn't have great technique or explosive punching power, but he learned how to fight by fighting.

Experience is just as important as practice and ability. Amateur boxing matches are only three three-minute rounds, meaning that in all of my thirteen one- or two-round victories combined, I got less than an hour of actual fighting time—not even close to the experience I needed to learn how to fight. This situation led to my second problem.

While knockouts entertain the crowd and empower the boxer, they don't develop a boxer's skills. None of my knockouts were the result of applying the sweet science. They were brutal displays of pugilistic power deployed against guys who lacked the talent to expose my weaknesses. My fifteenth amateur fight, against Fred Latham, displayed how little true boxing ability I had.

You Don't Know What You Don't Know

Fred had been boxing since childhood. I had only started boxing two years earlier. The difference in our experience levels was clear from the opening bell. I was never in danger of being hurt or knocked out, but he skillfully picked me apart by using his superior experience to stick and move. At several points in the fight, I swung with so much uncontrolled force that I slipped, effectively knocking myself down. I was swinging wide, missing wider, and, in the process, tripping over my own feet. I lost that fight.

After the loss, I started training with Chris Williams, a former standout local amateur boxer and a talented coach. Despite winning most of my fights with a knockout, anyone with eyes could see that I couldn't box. At best, I was street fighting with enough skill to beat anyone without training. At worst, I was a brawler, relying on sheer instinct, coasting on above-average athleticism, and surviving due to my high pain tolerance.

The overarching idea of the sweet science is for the fighter to hit and not get hit in return. I could hit guys, sure, but only if they hardly moved. And as for me not getting hit, well, that's why I was losing. If a fighter can't move and adequately maintain his balance while doing so, he can't properly adjust to his opponent's movements. Each step will cover too much space, or not enough, or be in the wrong direction. Chris spent weeks teaching me the most fundamental thing about boxing: footwork.

Every morning, Chris would drill me for hours on basic footwork patterns. I'd walk forward, backward, and to each side, careful to never cross my feet or step too wide. After I learned how to walk, we took things up a notch. He started teaching me how to shift my weight to quickly pivot and turn angles. Only after I mastered these skills did we add punching.

Another benefit of improved footwork is that it automatically increases your punching power. When a fighter has proper footwork and sound mechanics, his punches are always delivered from a balanced position. And because the fighter is punching with balance, he expends less energy trying to get himself back on balance to punch again. This efficiency gives him more energy to land more powerful shots.

I was already knocking guys out, but with proper footwork and balance, I could more quickly deliver greater force, which equated to more knockouts. Also, I was no longer getting tired in fights now that my body was moving more efficiently. I was doing more with less, and my improvement soon became evident.

My first fight with Chris Williams as my coach was a rematch against Wesley Triplett, the six-foot-six, 230-pound 2008 Cleveland Golden Gloves super heavyweight champion. Triplett was my first loss, even before my embarrassing defeat at the hands of Latham. Not only did I lose our first matchup, it was a minor miracle that he didn't knock me out.

In our rematch, I used my much-improved footwork to get myself into position to deliver a crushing overhand right. I stayed balanced, ducked my head to make him miss, and delivered the knockout punch as a skillful counterattack. I'm normally an emotionally reserved guy, but I was so excited that I jumped in the air right after the referee waved his hands, signaling the end of the match.

I was learning the sweet science. Although I had once again won by knockout, I felt like I was developing enough tools to be able to win on those occasions when I couldn't just put a guy to sleep.

The Only Way to Get a Different Outcome Is to Do Things Differently

After I beat Triplett in our rematch, I assumed I would have the same positive result when I fought a rematch against Fred Latham.

On a cold January 2011 evening, Latham and I met for the second time. This time, I didn't trip over my feet, and I pressed him against the ropes to deliver some brutal body shots. He still evaded my power punches, but he had to be more careful. Instead of falling on my ass after missing my shot at taking his head off, I stayed on my feet, still in position to make him pay.

There were moments in the fight when I thought I had him hurt. But while he bent, he did not break. The match was much closer than our first fight, but Fred still came out on top. On the drive home, I reflected on why I came up short again, despite having dynamite in my hands and polishing up my fundamentals.

The thing is, as your skills develop, you don't just get better. You also become better able to recognize not just your own weaknesses but the weaknesses of your peers and competitors. You go from knowing nothing to knowing enough to ask the questions that get you closer to the solution. You can recognize wrong answers, even if you don't know the correct ones.

The Four Levels of Competence, a learning model described by management coach Martin M. Broadwell in the 1960s, explains this progression. The model relates to the psychological states that a person passes through during their journey from beginner to expert.

The first and lowest level of skill acquisition is unconscious incompetence. At this stage:

1. The individual doesn't know how to do something.

2. They're unaware of their lack of knowledge or skill.

3. They "don't know what they don't know."

This stage is natural when starting to learn any new skill. However, it often lasts longer than people expect. Even after learning a few basic techniques, a person may remain at this level because:

1. They can only apply these techniques in familiar situations.

2. Their actions are mere reactions to known stimuli.

3. They lack a deeper understanding of the skill.

For example, a beginner chef might learn to follow a simple recipe but remain unaware of the principles behind cooking techniques or flavor combinations. They don't yet know enough to recognize how much more there is to learn.

Before training with Chris to develop my footwork and understand positioning, I was at the level of unconscious incompetence. I didn't even realize there was more to boxing than just trying to knock a guy out. I could hit my opponent, just as I had rehearsed on the heavy bag and mitts thousands of times—as long as he didn't move around the ring. I could punch, but only as a reactive recall in a predictable situation. The slightest deviation in my opponent's movement and position caused me to come undone. I was an incompetent boxer, but I thought I knew something about boxing because I'd had some knockout victories. I didn't. I was ignorant, and worse, I didn't even know it.

Chris's training and the experience I gained from sixteen fights brought me to the next level: conscious incompetence. At this level, an individual still doesn't understand or know much, but they're aware enough to know what they need to learn to get to the next level. If you aren't able or willing to see what's wrong, then there's no way you can do anything to improve. Conscious incompetence makes you honest about your inadequacies and motivates you to fix them.

Conscious incompetence is the level I was at following my second fight with Fred Latham. In our first fight, I was barely a novice and had the accompanying overconfidence typical of those still in the unconscious incompetence phase. Now, I knew enough to understand why I'd lost our first match and had a strategy to win our second.

The fight was much closer than before, but Fred still won decisively. Although I lost, I knew that I was close to beating him. I didn't feel he was much better than me anymore, but I knew he was doing something better. I knew I could improve, but I didn't yet see how.

I understood that Chris knew more about boxing than I did, but aside from the improvements in my footwork, I didn't feel like I was getting better. This stagnation made me reconsider training with him, which isn't unusual after a fighter suffers a loss. I went back and forth on what to do next, but circumstances beyond my control forced me to decide on the future of my training.

Don't Stop Looking Until You Find the Right Help

Fred Latham bounced among different trainers. At the time of our second fight, he was coached by J. Major "Philly" Medlin.

Philly was a likable guy; he once drove me to Washington, DC, and worked my corner for an amateur fight. But he didn't have a gym. Philly was a genuinely good guy, so when he needed a place to train Fred, Carrick Community Boxing Academy—where I trained with Chris—was happy to help him.

Sharing gym space with a rival was not a problem by itself. The problem was that boxing trainers typically train fighters in the evening, because they have day jobs, so Fred was training there at the same time I was. That was unacceptable, especially considering our third fight was less than three months away, at the national Golden Gloves regional qualifier.

By this point, I knew enough about boxing to know that if I wanted any chance of a real future in this game, I needed to get to the national level. If I wasn't good enough to defeat an average boxer from Pittsburgh, how would I ever stand a chance as a professional boxer? I wanted to get to the national level, and I would do whatever I thought would help me achieve that goal. That meant I needed to straighten out my training.

After my first few knockout victories as an amateur boxer, finding opponents to fight was difficult—but finding sparring partners was next to impossible.

Sparring can be intense, but it's safer than a competitive boxing match. Fighters use gloves with more cushion, which lessens the impact of punches that are already being thrown with less speed because the gloves weigh more. In sparring, when you land a shot that knocks the wind out of your opponent and makes his legs wobble, you don't move in for the kill. If a guy is hurt, pinned against the ropes, and unable to return shots, you step back and allow him to regain his bearings. Unless you're paying sparring partners to help you prepare for a professional bout, sparring is a classroom where fighters sharpen their technique and hone their timing against a live target. But despite this unwritten code of sparring that every fighter follows, many amateur fighters in my city were not interested in sparring with me, because I had won all of my fights by knockout.

The next issue was the small number of guys available to spar with me at my weight. Boxing is divided into weight classes. Other than heavyweight, each weight class has an upper limit; these divisions minimize size advantages and make the fights more competitive. I was a heavyweight, which meant that the lightest opponent I could face was 202 pounds. Of the guys available to spar with me in my city, most would eventually be forced to face me because there weren't that many heavyweights. This made the ones courageous enough to spar with me reluctant because we'd eventually compete against each other.

The final issue was the most ridiculous one: Personal politics between coaches sometimes kept fighters from getting better. There were times when a guy was ready, willing, and able to spar with me, even if we'd eventually fight each other in the ring, but the sparring couldn't happen because the coaches didn't like each other.

This combination of factors made it difficult to get sparring practice, and without sparring, it's impossible to improve. It doesn't matter how many miles you run, how many rounds you hit the mitts, or how long you hit the heavy bag. You can only get better at fighting if you practice fighting.

One of my first coaches, Ted Mrkonja, understood this and did whatever he could to find sparring opportunities for me. We once drove thirty miles north of Pittsburgh to Tom Yankello's World Class Boxing Gym so that I could spar with Andres "Taylor Made" Taylor, a cruiserweight professional fighter. I was impressed by the way Tom coached Andres during the sparring session. He stood in the ring with us, careful never to interfere, but instructing his fighter to break down my defense with efficient offensive maneuvers.

The next time I saw Tom was a sparring night at Carrick, when all of the fighters from his gym came down. They all were sharp, moved well, and had excellent punching ability. Tom wasn't in the ring this time, but he was on the sidelines, giving top-notch instruction and insight. By this point in my boxing journey, I'd seen enough sparring and fights to recognize these guys knew something that the other fighters in the area did not.

When I chose to leave Carrick, I wouldn't train with just anyone. By now, I understood that training requires more than just a guy with time, willingness, and experience in the ring. My initial coaches had those traits, but, while important, they do not get a fighter to the next level. I needed a trainer with a proven record of success. I thought back to that day when I watched the fighters from Tom Yankello's gym spar and started researching him.

When I asked around, no one gave a glowing recommendation for World Class Boxing. The one thing that kept coming up was that training up there would cause me to get hurt because the fighters sparred a lot and the training was too much. Because I was committed to being the best fighter I could become, this only made Yankello's gym even more attractive to me. However, working hard for its own sake is pointless if the work doesn't produce results. Despite all the criticism about the level of work or the intensity of sparring at the gym, no one ever mentioned the results of Tom's approach or methods. To get the answer to that question, I had to consult the internet.

In 2011, the first thing that came up when you searched for Tom Yankello was his work with 49–1–1 Paul Spadafora, the former International Boxing Federation (IBF) lightweight champion who made seven successful defenses of his title. Though Tom didn't work with Paul during his amateur career, he developed him throughout his professional career. Tom would later explain to me that many people thought he got lucky. Most coaches never get a fighter who wins a major belt, let alone one who defends it seven times and wins his first forty-eight fights. Tom was only twenty-eight when Paul won the title, so naturally, coaches who'd been around longer attributed his success to luck—but you're only lucky if you do it once. Under Tom's tutelage from the start of his amateur career, Verquan Kimbrough won the 2002 United States men's lightweight championship. (He'd repeat this feat with Kiante Irving, who won the national Golden Gloves middleweight championship in 2018.)

Though people told me that amateur boxing is a different animal than professional boxing, Tom had notable success at both levels. He'd trained Calvin Brock to a heavyweight title fight against Wladimir Klitschko and had gotten Monty Meza-Clay an International Boxing Association title. He had also gotten Kimbrough a pair of boxing titles as a professional. Tom's success as a trainer is so renowned that when the Boxing Writers Association of America's Fighter of the Decade Roy Jones Jr. sought a new trainer after he and his dad split, he found Tom Yankello.

Aside from the championships, Tom's stable of current and past fighters at the time I researched him included many with notable accomplishments who spent their entire careers with him. Between the success of his fighters and the grumblings I heard about the training, I knew Tom's gym was the place for me.

However, there would be some difficulties that I had to handle first.

To Make Progress, You Must Take Risks. To Take Risks, You Must Have Courage.

Despite all of my research into Tom, I still had my reservations.

What if he was just getting lucky? What if the training was too difficult or we didn't get along?

I worried that if I left Carrick and things didn't work out at World Class Boxing, I'd have nowhere to train. In retrospect, this was a silly fear, as I had a reputation for being a hard worker who was always game to fight and had knockout power. Any gym would have been happy to have me. However, I still wanted to leave myself with a safety net in case Tom was a fraud. So, I decided to train at both gyms. I trained in the morning at World Class and in the evening at Carrick.

This was a bad idea for multiple reasons. One, you only have so much energy. Two training sessions per day is not a bad idea by itself—I got in twice the repetitions—but this was the only positive aspect of my double life. I also worked three nights a week, from 7:00 p.m. to 7:00 a.m., at a men's homeless shelter. The job wasn't physically demanding, but working the graveyard shift takes a toll on your body. For those three days, I slept two hours after work (if I bothered to sleep at all), then went to World Class Boxing to train in the afternoon.

Boxing is more than bashing heads. It requires skills and techniques and relies heavily on reflexes and reactions. Without sleep, your learning aptitude, information retention, reaction speed, and neuromuscular coordination diminish significantly. So on the one hand, I practiced twice a day, which enabled me to make progress quickly, as I received feedback and reps from two teachers. On the other hand, I spent half the week exhausted and the other half catching up to the effects of that exhaustion.

Another major issue was transportation. World Class Boxing Gym was thirty miles north of where I lived, accessible only by a sporadically running bus. Fortunately, I had a car, but it was far from reliable. The car had no horn or seat belts and broken hazard lights. The brakes barely worked, the shocks were shot, the frame was rusted, and the electrical system would randomly fail—though, thankfully, the engine still ran. These problems made the car fail inspection, which is required annually in Pennsylvania to ensure safety. Mechanics focused on dangers to others on the road, like nonworking brakes or improper tires, while issues like faulty seat belts were considered my concern. Fixing the car would cost around three thousand dollars, but even then, it wouldn't pass inspection due to the rusted frame.

I managed to get essential parts—brakes, shocks, and tires—

through a friend whose family owned an auto-parts store. I skipped repairs for the heating and air-conditioning because I couldn't afford them and knew the car still wouldn't pass inspection if they were fixed. I just needed it to be safer to drive.

Another problem was that a car that fails inspection is uninsurable. I could afford the thirty-four-dollar monthly premium for the minimum required liability coverage, but this was irrelevant, since the car wasn't legally roadworthy. On top of that, an eighteen-month suspension of my license for unpaid traffic violations meant that even if the car passed inspection and I had insurance, I *still* couldn't legally drive.

To reach the next level of my training, I'd have to drive sixty miles daily on a well-policed stretch of highway, in a car that had failed inspection, without a license or insurance. If I got pulled over, I was definitely going to jail. Still, despite the risk, this was a bet I was willing to make. I wanted to reach my full potential as a boxer, and I felt that Tom Yankello was the trainer who could help me do that.

To avoid getting pulled over, I did all the standard stuff: I drove within the speed limit, kept my phone out of my hand, and never tried to beat the yellow lights. This ensured that the cops never had a reason to pull me over—but I also needed a strategy in case they pulled up behind me.

While the police would only know that I was driving with a suspended license if they pulled me over, one only had to pull up behind me to see that I didn't have registration stickers on my license plate. Now that everything is computerized, vehicles in Pennsylvania no longer put these stickers on the license plate, but in 2011, not having this sticker on display—or having one that was out of date—was an easy way to get pulled over. Also, the mechanic who passes your car for inspection puts a sticker on the lower left windshield with the date and the year's color code. Any officer who glanced at my car for a few seconds would see it hadn't been inspected. That would result in me getting pulled over, leading to the discovery of all the other laws I was breaking. I could not let that happen.

I trained myself to look at all the cars behind me, not just the ones directly behind me, to spot any police cars on the road. In case I spotted one, I made sure I knew all the places I could pull off the road without looking suspicious. It raises alarms if you suddenly pull off on a side street when the cops are behind you, but it's far less alarming if you pull into a gas station, drive-through, or convenience store, especially if you do it before they're directly behind you.

I'm happy to report that while I drove that car—which I affectionately called "jailbait"—twice a day for four months, I never once got pulled over.

Mental Rehearsal Leads to Flawless Physical Execution

Despite the many challenges, I began my training at World Class Boxing. I quickly discovered why Tom's training produced so many skilled fighters—and why so many fighters found it daunting. The rule at World Class was that for the entire time I was in the gym, I had to be busy. This meant shadowboxing, hitting the heavy bag, or working on the mitts. Tom's philosophy was that he would refine your technique by working with you on hitting the paddles. You'd train your physical abilities by hitting the bag and integrate it all together in a simulated fight by shadowboxing.

With Tom, I learned how to use the heavy bag as a tool for my cardiovascular conditioning. I worked the heavy bag with the same intensity as in a fight. Even at this intensity, Tom was still there to correct the errors in my punching technique or body positioning. After all, there is no point in practicing hard if you practice the wrong thing.

Tom taught me to shadowbox the same way: I imagined being in a real live fight, working distance, bobbing and weaving against an imaginary opponent. You might wonder what good fighting an imaginary opponent can do, but countless research studies have consistently reaffirmed the remarkable influence of visualization and mental imagery—the skills at the heart of shadowboxing—on physical performance. Multiple results have demonstrated that visualization can enhance physical ability, even without physical training.

In addition to the imaginary fighting, Tom had a massive library of VHS tapes of thousands of real fights he'd recorded. We'd spend hours watching tapes of fights like Tua vs. Ibeabuchi, Frazier vs. Ali, Qawi vs. Holyfield, and any other great fight that he thought represented the style that would suit me best in the ring. Tom understood the value of mental training, and he stressed it almost as much as he did the physical work.

Shadowboxing and studying film were just the tip of the iceberg. Pad work sessions were where the bulk of my development came from. During pad work, the coach holds the pads up to hit, allowing the boxer to refine their punching technique and drill combinations. It's a fundamental component of boxing training, simulating real-life punching scenarios and improving hand-eye coordination and footwork while training defensive maneuvers.

We drilled combinations for hours. I took breaks when I needed them, only long enough to get a swig of water but never long enough to catch my breath properly. This was part of the magic of the training: Even when I was fatigued, we pushed through it, because the only rest you can safely take in a fight is the one-minute break between rounds.

In psychology, there is a concept known as "overlearning." Overlearning is the process of practicing a skill beyond the point of mastery. It involves continuing to rehearse and repeat the skill even after learning it proficiently. Overlearning aims to solidify and automate the ability, making it more intuitive and difficult to forget. At this level of learning, training becomes a monotonous grind. However, I'm convinced that the only way to develop proficiency in anything is to practice to the point of boredom. Consistency and repetition only get you an invite to the audition. If you want the leading role, you need to know your craft so well that you don't think about it but could never forget it.

This work rate isn't unique to Yankello's training, but it was my first exposure to it. Any boxing gym with serious amateur or professional fighters has similar intensity. Every time you step through the ropes, even in sparring, there is a chance that you can sustain an injury that forever changes your life negatively. Boxing isn't play; it's serious business. Preparation for an event of this magnitude demands unwavering concentration, because in the ring, you don't rise to the level of the occasion—you fall to the level of your preparation. If you can execute accurately when you're tired, then you'll be unstoppable when your energy levels are high.

Exhaustion Makes You Weak, and Weakness Makes You Exhausted

Reaching Broadwell's third level of competence—conscious competence—requires more than just trying new things. It takes thinking in new ways about things you've always been doing. One of Tom's first critiques of my skills was of my punching power—the one thing I thought I had going for me. I was pummeling the heavy bag, and he watched me for about a minute before interrupting.

"You hit hard, but it's not even close to what you can do. Right now, they're all arm punches."

"Huh?" I looked at him for further clarity, too exhausted to form a complete sentence.

"You have power, but once we fix your balance and start putting your body behind shots, you'll really start hurting guys."

I knew my balance was weak, but this was the first time I'd heard of the idea of "arm punches." I nodded and returned to hitting the bag before he added one more thing.

"You're fast, too, but it doesn't mean anything if you can't see what you hit."

He was referring to my tendency to lower my head or look away from the target when I attacked. As an early amateur, you can get away with this, but better competition will make you pay for it with a nasty counterattack you won't see coming. Punches you don't see coming do the most damage, especially when you believe you won't get hit, which is how many fighters feel when they're in the middle of an attack.

Tom's corrections of my technique made me feel like I hadn't learned anything in my previous three years of boxing, but his approach to my physical conditioning was where I truly began to feel like I was learning the sport from scratch.

Above all other things, boxing is a skill sport. Many people erroneously believe that it's just a sport of brutality and aggression. This may be true, but without developing the proper skills and technique, it's no different than a street fight. Most street fights are unskilled scuffles. The fighters are swinging wildly, which is expected because they aren't trained. But you might not expect how little stamina they have—they burn out incredibly fast. A popular saying in boxing circles is that "skills pay the bills," but those skills are useless if you're too exhausted to execute.

That's why, every other day, he'd have me hop on the treadmill. He would take it to ten miles per hour, the maximum speed. I had to run at that pace for three minutes, the length of a boxing round, and then hop off for a one-minute rest. Although my coach designed the exercise to simulate a boxing match, we usually completed four or five rounds, exceeding the three rounds that amateur boxing matches last.

No matter how well you scout your opponent, you never know how tough he will be. Developing your capacity to do more than expected is an insurance policy against the unexpected. But really, the most significant benefit is psychological. When Vince Lombardi said, "Fatigue makes cowards of us all," the idea was that your ability to deal with challenging situations is inversely related to your energy levels. Everything is more difficult when you're tired, especially a fight. When you're used to running on a treadmill at top speed, fully aware that one slip means you fly off, the fatigue of a fight won't stand a chance against your resolve.

After a month of training at World Class, I was clearly improving. I hadn't ended my training at Carrick, and one day Chris commented on how much sharper my hook had become, still unaware that I was training elsewhere. It felt like I was cheating on my girlfriend. But in the end, this issue resolved itself.

The boxing community is remarkably well connected. Everyone talks, and everyone knows one another. Word eventually got back to Chris and Carrick that I was going to World Class Boxing. I remember the day I woke up from sleeping after my night shift at the homeless shelter to an angry text from Chris: "After everything Scott and me did for you to help you train, you got a lot of balls training up at Tom's. You're no longer welcome at Carrick Boxing."

I felt bad because he was right. Scott Bradley was a patron who was paying Chris for the time he was putting in working with me every morning on my footwork. They justifiably felt betrayed, not just because I was training at another gym but because I was doing it so sneakily. I should have properly ended things with one gym before training at another. Today, Chris and I are friends who have mutual respect for each other, but he was right. I had behaved like a man without honor. I wanted to shield myself from the risk of leaving my previous boxing gym because, ironically enough, I was terrified of the conflict.

Returning to the analogy of a relationship: I didn't have the heart to say to Chris that we should go our separate ways and start seeing other people. Instead, I just grew distant and started cheating. And, like most cheaters, I was relieved when I finally got caught.

Getting thrown out of Carrick meant my energy levels were no longer an issue, so we could really step up my training at World Class. I could spend even more time at the gym, and so I learned even faster. My energy levels and skills were peaking just in time for my first fight in the Golden Gloves tournament, which would be my chance to finally put myself on the boxing map.

Small Improvements over Time Add Up to Big Results

The fourth level of competence is "unconscious competence." This level of intuition seems like precognition, but it's just the result of pattern recognition and grueling repetition.

Unconscious competence is essential in boxing because in a fight there is no time to think. You can get away with some thinking against weaker competition, but getting to the highest levels of the sport requires an instinctive mastery of your techniques and movement. Tom designed our training with this goal—to make me instinctive and reactive. That's why we drilled so often and so long. Amateurs practice until they get it right, but professionals practice until they can't get it wrong. Overlearning and overpracticing under stressful conditions prepare your mind to be disciplined, reactive, and accurate in the heat of battle.

My first fight with Tom as my coach was also my first fight of the 2011 Pennsylvania Golden Glove tournament. My opponent was Aaron Quattrocchi, a guy who'd barely made the heavyweight minimum of 201 pounds and who I'd never even heard of. This fight would be the first live test of my training.

It was the first time I felt I understood the sweet science. I used footwork to maneuver around my opponent, but because my balance had greatly improved, I was always in a position to hit and not get hit. But Quattrocchi was no slouch. He took shots that would have put down bigger men and did so with a smile.

If we had fought three months earlier, Quattrocchi would have beaten me. He wasn't more skilled than I was, but he was tough. For three rounds, he took my best punches—and they were significantly more powerful punches than my former arsenal because they came from a balanced base, with my body instead of my arms behind each shot. I couldn't knock him out, but this was fine, because my skills had improved so much that I won on points by a wide margin. I hit him so hard and frequently that it was the first time I ever had to ice my hands after a fight. I could always hit hard, but now I had the skill to go along with power punching, and that skill had carried me through the first round of the tournament.

The next fight was the third installment in the trilogy between Fred Latham and me. Rather than throwing power bombs and hoping for the best, I closed the ring off with footwork, preventing him from easily evading my shots and keeping him occupied with a constant jab in his face.

In the second round, he threw a crisp jab and tried to step back out of range of my counterattack. He got out of the way of my first attempt, but I put him in a position where he couldn't back up a second time, because my footwork forced his back to the corner post. He wasn't aware of his position, but I was, so when he stepped back, there was nowhere to go but into my right hook.

A loud *crack* reverberated through the arena when my punch cleanly connected with Latham's chin. He tried to fire back but was hurt and off-balance this time. Without thinking, I immediately followed up with another powerful right hook. This one dropped him to the canvas, flat on his back. He got to his feet, but his legs wobbled like Jell-O. The ref didn't like how he looked, so ten seconds into the second round, he waved his hands above his head, signaling that the fight was over. I defeated my old rival by a second-round stoppage.

While my victory proved that I had gained a deeper understanding of the sweet science, there were still doubts about whether I had gotten better or had just gotten lucky. In a few weeks, I'd face a test that would alter the course of my boxing career—and my entire life. I would also gain a much greater appreciation of luck's role in our successes and failures.

VI

The Harder You Work,
the Luckier You Get

Two weeks after I defeated Fred Latham, I beat the champion from Philadelphia to become the 2011 Pennsylvania Golden Gloves champion for the over-201-pounds weight division. I was never in danger of losing or getting seriously hurt, but I could hardly celebrate afterward because the inside of my mouth got cut up pretty badly during the fight. Still, I drank and partied anyway because my victory meant that, in two weeks, I'd be fighting at the Golden Gloves National Tournament of Champions in Indianapolis, as the heavyweight representative for Pennsylvania. I had far exceeded expectations for someone learning the sweet science at my age.

Everyone in the boxing community made a big deal about the Golden Gloves; one common bragging point for guys who used to fight is that they were Golden Gloves boxers. Most of the time, they just mean they competed in their local-level tournament. Rarely did I meet someone who had won their state title and went on to compete at the national level. As there is only one champion crowned per state in each weight class, there aren't that many champions. I was now one of them, and that was an incredible feeling, but that wasn't even the best part.

The best part was seeing how my hard work and instincts had paid off. I had trained hard to accomplish this. I bet on myself and took a chance by changing trainers and training methods. It was the first time in my life that I earned something on the strength of my work ethic and by trusting my intuition, and I was just getting started. The next step was proudly representing Pennsylvania in the national Golden Gloves tournament.

We were Team Pennsylvania, a mix of champions from Pittsburgh and Philadelphia, and we landed in the Circle City on April 24, 2011. Eager to prove our worth against other champions representing their respective states—or, in the case of sparsely populated states, clusters of states grouped under one banner—we immediately checked into our hotel rooms at the J. W. Marriott before registering with the tournament directors.

Back then, that was the nicest hotel I had ever stayed in. The Golden Gloves of America covered our plane tickets and hotel costs and gave us a fifty-dollar meal stipend daily. The money wasn't much, but it was better than having to cover the cost of three meals out of pocket, especially considering that most boxers—especially amateurs who don't compete for money—are poor.

And at that moment, I was even poorer than usual.

Money Doesn't Buy Happiness, but It Can Keep You from Being Miserable

The week before I left for the tournament, my roommate informed me he was moving out. He was a college kid, so his father was our apartment's credit application cosigner. If I wanted to stay, I'd have to apply as a new applicant to take over the lease. As much as I liked living at the heart of all the college parties and bars in the neighborhood, this meant I'd have to leave.

At the time, I had a credit score of 420. That's so bad that even a cosigner with perfect credit wouldn't make much of a difference. And even if I did find someone with a decent credit rating to co-sign, and a landlord willing to rent to me, my only source of income was a paltry $7.25 per hour from my job at Starbucks. Most rentals require applicants to have an income of three times the monthly rent. Even working overtime, minimum wage wasn't going to cut it.

Boxing wasn't helping with that part of my life. I was still an amateur. This fighting status meant I couldn't earn any money for fighting. When most people think of boxing, the image that comes to mind is of the guys who fight on TV. These are professional boxers, so they get paid to punch each other; that's why boxers are also known as "prizefighters." Floyd Mayweather Jr. said it best when a reporter accused him of picking opponents based not on skill or ranking but on their ability to sell a fight and their fan base. "What do you think we do this for?" he said. "We're prizefighters. We fight for prizes."

Even if I started competing at the professional level then and there, it would take months to get my first fight, and the earnings from it would be laughably low. To give you an idea of how little boxers make at the start of their professional careers, consider the following: My first six professional boxing matches each earned me less than eight hundred dollars—before I paid trainer fees and taxes. Fighting wasn't going to solve my immediate financial problems.

As I walked around the Marriott, admiring its fancy decor and examining the massive convention center attached to it where the bouts would be held, I tried to put my money troubles out of my mind and focus on the tournament. For a moment, I felt like I had finally arrived, but I quickly got my head back in the game and remembered that I hadn't accomplished anything yet. This trip wasn't a vacation; it was a mission. However, the first order of business was entirely out of my hands: the draw.

To determine the initial tournament pairings, the Golden Gloves organizers randomly draw fighter names and match them up over five grueling days. A single loss eliminates the boxer; the luck of the draw decides his opponent. The tournament format could match a fighter against the best boxer in the country, or against someone who became the regional champion only because no one else in their weight class entered from that region.

A crowd gathered in one of the hotel conference rooms to witness the drawing, but I consciously decided to stay away. My rationale was simple: I couldn't control who I'd face in the ring, so there was no point in watching. I wouldn't hear a name drawn and decide to back out and, if my opponent was good enough to make it to the national finals, nor would he. It's different in lower-level local amateur bouts, where a fighter backing out at the last minute is a surprisingly common occurrence. There are no cowards at the national level.

Later that night, one of my teammates told me that my first fight would be against Dominic Breazeale, the champion from California. I had yet to look online for any information about him. Now that I knew, I tried to resist the temptation, but my curiosity got the best of me: Before turning in for the night, I started researching my opponent. I stayed up until midnight, scouring Google and YouTube for information about him. What struck me instantly was his towering height—a daunting six foot seven. At that height, he'd be incredibly strong and powerful—and longer arms meant greater reach. They could keep a fighter like me, only six foot one, at bay and allow him to deliver powerful blows from a safe distance.

Dominic's credentials spoke volumes about his exceptional athleticism. He was a former starting quarterback at the University of Northern Colorado. After graduating, he had bounced around a few NFL camps before taking up boxing. Being the champion of California, the most populous state in the country, also meant he'd had access to a vast pool of talent, sparring partners, and top-notch training opportunities. He had even faced other national champions, like four-time Golden Gloves and five-time national champion Cam Awesome. My most challenging opponent thus far had been Fred Latham, and it took me three tries to beat him. (A few weeks after the Golden Gloves tournament, Dominic would go on to dominate Fred Latham, stopping him halfway through the third round.)

His path to the national tournament had also been considerably more challenging than mine, since California's larger population meant greater competition. Generally speaking, the winner of a competition with more competitors will be better than one with fewer entrants. I'd only had to fight three times to win the Pennsylvania Golden Gloves. Dominic had fought seven times to win California.

These facts didn't keep me up at night. Instead, they fueled my excitement for the challenge ahead. I had a mission: to prove to myself and my local boxing community in Pittsburgh that my victory over Latham wasn't just a one-off. This fight would test my hard work and dedication, and I was eager to embrace it head-on— to prove that I wasn't just lucky.

Most People Miss Their Lucky Break Because It's Disguised as a Tough One

The tournament began the evening after the draw. The bouts in amateur shows typically run sequentially, from lightest to heaviest weight class, meaning I fought near midnight. The referee introduced us. I was first to be called to the center of the ring. When the referee introduced me over the loudspeaker, I walked up to him and nodded.

Looking at Dominic in the opposing corner, I was amazed at how much larger than me he was. At six foot one and 230 pounds, I'm hardly a small man. However, sharing the ring with Dominic, I looked tiny. Before that moment, I don't think I'd ever seen someone six foot seven, and I'd definitely never fought someone that tall. When he came to the center of the ring, he raised his hands in an arrogant assumption of victory. Since he was armed with an 81.5-inch wingspan—nearly seven feet—this gesture further exaggerated our height difference.

As he towered above me, his fists in the air, I looked him up and down and immediately thought of the biblical story of David and Goliath. In the story, a young shepherd named David takes on the Philistine giant Goliath, who is heavily armed and fearsome. Despite his small size and lack of combat experience, David slays the giant using a perfectly aimed slingshot to hit him right between the eyes, his only vulnerable area. Dominic was the battled-hardened Goliath, the California team, the Philistine, and I the lone shepherd, defiantly stepping forth to slay the giant on behalf of Pennsylvania.

I didn't feel overmatched, underprepared, or intimidated—just small.

When the bell rang, though, my thoughts about the man in front of me fell silent. He was no longer six foot seven; he was no longer 250 pounds. I forgot where he was from, his accomplishments, and his athletic credentials. He became just another obstacle to overcome, an opponent to face and a chip to knock off my shoulder.

Because Dominic was so much taller than me and possessed a longer wingspan, he used his jab to keep me from getting close enough to hit him. When I managed to get in range, he would lean on me, forcing me to expend extra energy to break free and maneuver into an ideal position to punch. My strategy for dealing with this size mismatch was simple: take his advantage and turn it into a weakness. Using my jab, head movement, and footwork, I slipped inside his range and punished his body and head with hooks.

My training with Tom had improved my skills, but he had also been careful not to take away my basic instincts and natural inclinations as a fighter. One of my greatest assets was a refusal to be pushed around or bullied in a fight: "You don't know how to take a step backward" is how Tom would say it. This assessment wasn't a criticism. It was recognition of a valuable innate trait you can't teach fighters: courage. If a boxer's fighting style is a mismatch for his fighting abilities, he may take unnecessary damage. Tom didn't try to teach me a new style of boxing. Instead, he chipped away the extraneous, refined the imperfections, and optimized my strengths.

These modifications allowed me to maximize the damage I delivered while minimizing the punches I received. Whenever Dominic tried to impose his physicality on me, I put even more pressure on him. If he wanted to retreat to a safe distance, he would have to earn the space he put between us. I was trying to kill him, and the only way he was going to save his life was to end mine first.

He landed a few good shots, but the adrenaline made me impervious to their effects. I would either leave the ring victorious or make the paramedics on standby earn their paycheck. When the final bell rang, the entire Pennsylvania team gathered around and cheered. I could hear two of my best friends, Matt and Bill, who had driven from Pittsburgh to Indianapolis, hollering from the stands.

I left everything I had in the ring during that fight and felt I'd won. However, the ringside judges scoring the fight can some-times see things differently. While waiting for the final scores, I worried I had lost the fight in their eyes, even if the crowd's reac-tion told me otherwise. Finally came the verdict:

"Your winner, from the blue corner, Ed Latimore!"

I had won, but I was exhausted from fighting the battle of my life and doing it at such a late hour. By the time the judges read the scores, it was two minutes to midnight. I limped back to my hotel room to rest up for the next bout. Before I passed out, though, I made sure I posted on Facebook, so everyone back home knew I hadn't just gotten lucky.

Preparation Provides Opportunity; Opportunity Tests Preparation

The next night, I scored a 5–0 sweep against Cameron Glenn, from Michigan. With two national-level victories under my belt, I was feeling pretty confident. But my next opponent was Donovan Dennis, a crafty six-foot-four southpaw from Davenport, Iowa. I didn't even know Iowa had a boxing scene—but they sure pro-duced a remarkable fighter in Dennis.

Dennis hadn't won a national championship, but he was a na-tional and international boxing veteran. He'd already had more than a hundred amateur fights by the time we fought, twenty-three of which had been high-level tournament bouts. Every punch he landed was heavy and did not feel like it came from a guy who only weighed 215 pounds. The difference in our experience was too significant for me to overcome, and I lost the fight by a score of 0–5.

Knocked out of the tournament, I headed to the hotel restaurant with Matt and Bill. Their jobs had given them the flexibility to come see me fight, and I wanted to unwind with my friends.

"Looks like I figured out what to do when I can't just knock a guy out!" I said.

"You sure did, man. Great job," Matt replied with a smile.

Tom had also come to see the fight, even though he wasn't allowed in my corner. The Golden Gloves tournament rules permitted only state-designated coaches to corner fighters, but Tom came anyway to offer insights between bouts.

Dinner was a mix of unwinding with my friends and getting coached by Tom, who kept giving me feedback and pointers. At one point, I excused myself to use the bathroom. While I was at the urinal, I suddenly heard a voice, almost right over my shoulder.

"Hey, mate, that was fantastic! Spot-on job out there!"

"Uh, thanks, man . . ."

While I appreciated the compliment, this guy was breaking two unwritten rules of male bathroom behavior: (1) Strangers don't talk while standing at the urinal, and (2) keep your distance. Everyone knows that if a man is using the urinal and another urinal is free, you don't take the one next to him. Look, I don't make the rules, but every man knows them.

"I'm Paul Cain. What part of Pennsylvania you from, mate? Where'd you learn to box?"

He sounded like he was either British or Australian, so I figured that maybe bathroom etiquette was different where he was from.

"Pittsburgh," I said—not rudely, but in a way that made it clear I wasn't interested in carrying on a conversation in the bathroom. Aside from the violation of bathroom etiquette, I was trying to relax.

"Fantastic. After the fight you gave to Dominic, we've been following all of your fights to see how you performed. Great job, man. I got some people who wanna meet you, mate! We're having dinner right now. Come on!"

He didn't ask if I'd be interested. He just beckoned me to follow him as he left the restroom. Again, I chalked this up to cultural differences and went along.

I'd heard stories of promoters courting fighters at tournaments and did consider it might be one of those opportunities, but I'm also not delusional. While I had given a decent performance, there were still four heavyweight fighters in the tournament. Two of them—Donovan Dennis and Cam Awesome—were significantly more experienced and polished and had been fighting for years under the World Series of Boxing banner as "semi-professionals." If these guys were indeed promoters, they had brighter prospects.

Those thoughts tumbled through my head as I followed this stranger out of the restroom to a round table in the hotel restaurant. Five men were seated at the table, all laughing at something. Then Paul introduced me. "Look at who I found in the bathroom! This is Ed Latimore, the guy who beat Dominic. Ed, this is Prentiss, Dave, Tommy, Henry, and Michael King."

Michael was the only guy whose last name he gave. I nodded and shook everyone's hand.

"I was just telling Ed how we watched his fights after he beat Dom because we'd never seen him before."

I'd later learn this meant that there was no tape circulating on the internet of my previous fights, and they had no intel on me because it was the first time I'd made it to the national level.

"Yeah, you really gave Dominic problems in there that we weren't expecting. Good job. Who's your coach?"

"Tom Yankello. He's right over there."

I called out to Tom to come over, and he introduced himself. Then Michael King started talking.

"Dominic's been with us the longest out in California. We run a program called All-American Heavyweights. We're taking former Division-I athletes from other sports and training them to be boxers. We're trying to get one to the Olympics. You should come out. We'll pay for your housing and food, and you'll also get a stipend."

"Sounds pretty good," I said. I wanted to sound sincere, but honestly, I didn't take these guys too seriously. I had no idea who they were, and they were intoxicated and rowdy, so even if they *were* serious, I doubted they'd remember me the next day. And hey, maybe they were giving all the boxers at the tournament the same spiel. Later, after exchanging numbers and saying our good-byes, I didn't expect to hear from them again.

The Chains of Addiction Are Too Light to Be Felt Until They Are Too Heavy to Be Broken

Now that the tournament was over, my first order of business was to get drunk. The best part was that the bars in Indiana closed at 3:00 a.m. instead of the usual 2:00 a.m. we were used to in Pennsylvania. My friends got the first few rounds of drinks, but when I tried to pay for a round, my bank card was declined.

At this point in my life, I was living on two income sources: one legal and the other, er, not so much. The thing was, I hadn't worked much the week before I left for the tournament, and anyway, that paycheck wasn't set to hit my account until the following week. However, I was still receiving unemployment benefits from a previous job. The extra money was the only way I made enough to pay my bills and put enough gas in my car to drive the sixty miles daily to and from Tom's gym.

I wasn't too worried. The money was usually deposited into my account at midnight, but it occasionally wouldn't show up until 7:00 a.m. the next day. Matt and Bill didn't let my lack of funds stop the good times and continued financing the night's festivities. I kept downing shots, determined to have a good time and enjoy my success on the national stage.

The evening started off great, but by the end of the night, I found myself on the phone, having a drunken argument with a friend over a girl I only thought about because I was drinking. I didn't even make it back to my bed, passing out in the hotel hallway instead. I woke up two hours later, just in time to avoid anyone from the tournament spotting me in my disheveled, drunken state.

Once I came to, I immediately called my friend to apologize profusely for my behavior. Unfortunately, this wasn't the first time I'd had to make amends for drunken calls and texts. With a sense of dread, I scrolled through my phone, piecing together the night through a trail of incoherent texts and regrettable social media posts. Apologizing to my friend wasn't the only thing I needed to worry about—I had also sent mass messages about how wasted I was and even texted an ex I hadn't spoken to in months.

I didn't feel embarrassed. I just didn't want people pissed off at me. My thinking was that as long as I blamed it on the alcohol, it was OK. This approach to dealing with drunken behavior is so common that "Blame It (On the Alcohol)" was the title of a hit song that spent fourteen weeks at number one on the Hot R&B/Hip-Hop Songs *Billboard* chart in the United States. The song's catchy beat is part of why it was so popular, but the message also resonated with the common experience of committing outlandish, offensive, and stupid behavior while intoxicated. But that was entertainment. In real life, people are not always easily forgiving.

My actions while under the influence were affecting my relationships, my reputation, and potentially my career. I had always prided myself on being responsible and disciplined in the ring, but alcohol was eroding my self-control and decision-making abilities outside of it.

The problem was that I believed drinking was a key part of my personality. It made me the life of the party. I was the guy everyone wanted to hang out with, because I was good at beating people up and I was down for drinking whenever, wherever, whatever, and as much as I could. To me, getting blackout drunk was not a bug in my psyche I needed to deal with. It was a feature that brought me even more attention on top of my boxing.

I knew my drinking could get out of control and cause problems, but I didn't feel any shame. I figured that if someone didn't like me when I was drinking, then we wouldn't get along when I was sober. Still, I did have a few reservations about it. I didn't go out of my way to hide it, but I was also aware of how at odds it was with my presentation as a serious athlete.

While many fighters drink and party and still manage to win fights, there's a cost to this lifestyle—especially when it spirals out of control. I was getting dangerously close to that point.

You Make Your Own Luck

After returning to Pittsburgh, I took a few days off before going back to the gym. I had fought three intense, highly competitive fights on three consecutive days, and my body needed time to recover. While recovering, I spent my time either looking for a higher-paying job or continuing the celebration with alcohol. It didn't matter that I didn't have any money. People were more than willing to buy me drinks at bars, and the booze at parties was free anyway.

Five days later, I returned to the gym. The first thing Tom wanted to know was if I had talked with those guys from California.

"No," I said. "I didn't think they were serious anyway."

"Well, they're serious. They've been blowing up my phone all week. I told them I'd let you know when you got back to the gym."

Tom gave me the phone number of their recruitment liaison, Joe Oniwor.

"So you're the guy that took Dominic to school, eh?"

"I don't know about all that. That was the hardest fight I've ever had."

"Ha ha, well, it's good to be humble. What's your email address? I'm gonna send you over some forms to fill out before I can book your ticket. In the meantime, check out the website."

I had to jot down my physical measurements, submit topless frontal and profile photos, and figure out my amateur boxing record. Then, I checked out the website for All-American Heavyweights (AAH). They were serious about finding "the next great American heavyweight."

AAH, I learned, was the dreamchild of media mogul Michael King. When King died in 2015, *The New York Times* wrote, "On a typical day in the late 1980s, 90 million people watched at least one of the company's three biggest shows—'Wheel of Fortune,' 'Jeopardy!' and 'The Oprah Winfrey Show.'"

King's media experience and passion for boxing made him frustrated with the lagging American interest in the sport. In the 1960s and '70s, major networks regularly showed boxing for free. Eventually, cable networks began showing fights on their premium channels, which meant that fans had to pay a premium price—not just to watch *HBO Boxing After Dark* or Showtime's *ShoBox* but also to watch big fights that came on pay-per-view. These price barriers eliminated most casual fans, but the sport still had bankable consumer interest. The nail in the coffin would be the changes in other sports.

In 1970, the average salary in MLB was $20,000. In 2005, the average jumped to $2.6 million. In 1964, Jim Brown's $50,000 salary made him the highest-paid player in the NFL. In 2017, the NFL minimum salary for a rookie was $465,000, and the average salary was $2.25 million. In 1970, the average NBA salary was $35,000. By 2010, that average had skyrocketed to $4.9 million.

Compare these numbers to the state of boxing. On average, a boxer only makes $67,948 per year. That figure doesn't seem too bad until you realize the median boxing salary is $2,000. Big-money fighters like Canelo Álvarez and Anthony Joshua raise the average, but most fighters barely make enough to cover training, let alone make a living. If you're a kid with athletic promise, picking any other major American sport is an obvious choice. Even if you don't make it to the professional level, you might land a scholarship that sets you up to study something for a better life. And, because you didn't spend years taking punches to the head, you'll be able to use that scholarship.

Over time, American boxing lost the nation's biggest, strongest athletes to other sports that are less dangerous and have more benefits. Other countries didn't have this issue, as either they subsidized their amateur boxers' living expenses or the competing sports weren't enticing enough to lure would-be boxers away. As a result, Americans weren't competitive in the heavyweight division, typically the most popular and highest-earning section.

Michael King sought to resolve these issues, starting with the AAH program. He once told the Associated Press, "If I were selling

'Oprah' the way they're selling boxing, you wouldn't know her."
He created AAH to build a heavyweight star, plucking candidates
from the sports where he believed the best athletes were: football
and basketball. His vision was to sign fighters to the boxing promotion company he started, King Sports Worldwide. AAH was
where he planned to build his fighters' amateur careers before
turning them into pay-per-view stars. King's own fortune, and additional backing from former Nike CEO Phil Knight, businessman
Ron Burkle, and Nanci Chambers and David James Elliot—actors
from the hit television series *JAG*—gave him the financial muscle
to invest heavily in this dream.

The AAH website had an open application with three conditions: You needed to be a former Division-I athlete, taller than six
foot two, and younger than twenty-five. I'm six foot one and, at
the time, weighed 230 pounds. Compared to other humans, I'm
large, but by heavyweight standards, I'm miniscule. The average
heavyweight boxer is six foot four and 240 pounds, so it made
sense that AAH recruited from collegiate football and basketball
teams, where even the smallest athletes exceeded those metrics.

I had played some Division III college football—a far cry from
the athletic standard required to compete at the Division I level—
and looking over the roster and seeing the recruitment criteria, I
noted that I would also be the oldest athlete there. The program
recruited athletes right out of college, so most of them were under
twenty-three. At twenty-six, I wasn't ancient, but I was also not a
twenty-two-year-old fresh out of a Division I sports program.

In other words, I didn't fit *any* of their screening criteria. If I
had applied through their website, AAH would have rejected my

application. However, I had beaten Dominic Breazeale, their most experienced, physically imposing recruit, and I had done so in my first fight on the national level. After the tournament, they had seemed excited to meet me, and I had beaten their guy, proving that my age, height, and lack of Division I pedigree wasn't a hindrance. But I also remembered thinking they were drunk and not particularly serious, and since they still wanted me to fill out the application, I figured they could still reject me.

A few days later, my doubts vanished.

"Hey, Ed. Good news, man. You're in. We booked your ticket to get you out here this Sunday. That cool?" Joe still had the same cheerful tone as he did on our first call.

"No problem, man," I said, trying to play it cool. "Excited to meet you and everyone there."

I was happy to focus on my training and relieved to have a source of income and a place to live, even if it meant moving across the country on four days' notice. During my five-day break from the gym, I had learned my unemployment benefits had been terminated. So, the timing couldn't have been better.

In a short time, I had gone from being an obscure, club-level amateur boxer to being flown out to Los Angeles and getting my training sponsored, every amateur boxer's dream. Having your training sponsored meant that you were effectively a professional athlete. I still maintained amateur status, but now my only job would be to box.

Looking back on one of the most significant events in my life, I see that it came about through a blend of continuous hard work and incredible luck. It's impossible to give either one all the credit. Luck plays a significant role in the achievements of any successful person, but successful people don't like this idea; they believe that it detracts from the effort they put in. Most people view luck as something beyond their control, and as something that usually compensates for a lack of skill or ability. They feel that crediting any of their success to luck fails to recognize their hard work. In this way, they see luck and hard work as mutually exclusive. It becomes either "I got lucky" or "I worked hard."

The reality is that any significant accomplishment is a confluence of both individual effort and interference from factors beyond your control. You make your own luck, but paradoxically, only when you're acting in a way that reduces the need for luck. In this way, creating luck comes from strategic decisions that reduce uncertainty. The old saying "The harder I work, the luckier I get" perfectly encapsulates this reality.

At the 2011 Golden Gloves tournament, I had done the preparation. But I couldn't control the opportunity. When I drew Dominic Breazeale, I could've looked at it as bad luck: He was one of the best fighters in the tournament. Instead, I rose to the challenge, and the draw turned out to be lucky, in that it got the attention of the AAH team, who wouldn't have noticed me if I had faced an easier opponent. Who knows if another opportunity would've come up had that one not happened. The important thing is that when luck presented itself, I was ready for it. Now I had the chance to really change my life.

I was worried about going out to California and failing miserably. Everyone would be younger, stronger, and in better shape. It was a challenge I was up for, though, and I had earned it.

VII

You're Only as Good as Your Last Win

Because my fight against Dominic was my first fight at the national level, AAH was curious enough about my potential to bring me out to the program, but they weren't completely sold. They didn't waste any time discovering whether recruiting me was the right decision.

I landed in Los Angeles on May 23, 2011, and in six days, I had my first match against Ja-Boy Leomiti, a six-foot-three, 260-pound former linebacker hailing from the University of Texas at El Paso. He'd been with AAH for over a year and had twenty fights. It was also my first outdoor boxing match, with the event set up along the Venice Beach boardwalk.

I didn't fight a great fight, as I was still adjusting to the time zone difference, and I had spent most of the week getting medical clearances rather than training, but I won a convincing decision.

With AAH's curiosity temporarily satisfied, I spent the next few weeks getting adjusted to the training routine. Every morning, at 7:00 a.m., we met for cardio training. On Monday, Wednesday, and Friday, this was a four-mile run. On Tuesday and Thursday, we focused on sprints, plyometrics, and agility drills. Afterward, I returned to my apartment for breakfast and studied boxing films before heading to the gym to start practice at 9:00 a.m. We started the day with a brief warm-up before the training began. After training, there was lunch, and then the physical trainers ran us through a strength and mobility circuit.

At any given time, there were twenty to twenty-five guys in the program. To handle that number of athletes, multiple boxing trainers were required. Fighters were assigned to a trainer, and their victories were also the coach's victory, because the coaches were always potentially on the chopping block as well. Boxing is a zero-sum game, so someone has to lose every fight, but if a coach's fighters lost too many fights or weren't making satisfactory progress, the coach got fired.

When I arrived, I was assigned to John Hernandez Bray, a former national heavyweight boxing champion and Junior Olympic gold medalist. Bray was also a 2009 California Boxing Hall of Fame inductee who carried much respect in the California boxing community. His coaching style was slow and deliberate, focusing on punch selection and precision. His training sessions weren't physically taxing—they didn't have to be, because of the morning conditioning routine—but Bray was a perfectionist in his approach.

Two weeks after my fight against Ja-Boy in Venice Beach, with Bray in my corner, I fought Edwin Alvarez. Alvarez didn't have as much experience as me, but he was six foot seven, and Henry Tillman, the 1984 Olympic gold medalist in heavyweight boxing, was coaching in his corner. However, not only was I coached by John Bray, but Tom had flown in to check out the program and was also in my corner.

During a rough start in the first round, in which I had barely landed any punches, Tom noticed that Edwin let his hands and eyes follow wherever the punches went. This mistake is common with less experienced fighters and leaves them vulnerable. More experienced fighters know to focus on the chest, as all information about the punches thrown can be gleaned from there. Looking at your opponent's chest also keeps you from "getting caught looking" at decoy punches and feints, and it has the added benefit of keeping your chin down, making you harder to knock out.

Once a fighter recognizes that his opponent's attention follows whatever punches are thrown, or that he prematurely reacts to anything that looks like a punch, it's easy to exploit this mistake. The fighter simply throws a harmless-looking punch in one place and then quickly attacks the undefended area. Those were the instructions Tom gave me in between rounds.

The second round lasted only five seconds. I started by flicking out two jabs aimed at his chest. As Tom had noticed, Edwin's attention and defense followed those punches, leaving him open for a devastating overhand right. When it connected, he fell so quickly that his head hit the canvas before he did. He managed to stand up before the referee counted him out, but his legs were so wobbly that the referee immediately waved the fight off.

Edwin was held out of practice the following week to recover. Once he passed the neurological tests, he was given a plane ticket home and cut from the program. My spot in the program was assured, and I went out to celebrate by getting drunk, by myself, at a local bar and posting about my victory on social media.

It would have been nice to have friends, but I had no problem drinking by myself. After all, I had earned it.

You Can Only Go as Far as Your Biggest Weakness

While every fighter in the program had an apartment, we had to share it with another participant. We were grouped three to an apartment, but none of us minded—it was a free place to stay, and most of the guys were used to sharing a dorm room anyway.

I was placed into a room with Malagamali'i "Malanga" D'Hue and a guy I'll refer to as PR. Malanga was an inch taller than me but lighter. He told me that AAH was looking to focus on developing bigger guys, but he kept winning and excelled at the workouts, so they still hadn't found a reason to cut him. Considering his size, though, he knew he would be out of the program when he lost.

Malanga was easy to get along with because he was a genuinely funny guy. He approached people the same way he approached his position in the program: With no judgment, he took everyone as they came and enjoyed the moment. As I got to know other guys in the program, I only heard good things about Malanga. Unfortunately, he was cut from the program a month after I arrived. That meant that PR was my only roommate now.

Boxing is a tough business, and the way AAH structured its training was even tougher than it is for many professionals. Daily practice is standard, but a structured running and lifting program is more than what most amateur fighters are capable of on their own, due to limitations of time and money. AAH didn't have those restrictions, so we trained like it was a full-time job. This also meant a heavy dose of sparring.

The AAH gym, "the Rock," was spacious, with three Olympic-sized rings and twelve heavy bags. This was the only way to accommodate all the boxers training at once. We sparred three times a week, which greatly accelerated everyone's development but also put a lot of wear and tear on the boxers. To reduce the damage, the program had a few resident sparring partners. AAH didn't get the sparring partners any fights or force them to train with us, but they received accommodations and $1,200 per month. It wasn't a bad deal if you didn't want to compete in matches, but PR had greater ambition than being a sparring partner for amateur boxers—despite being thirty-four years old and having no amateur fights under his belt.

PR got his chance in August, at the 2011 national Ringside tournament in Kansas City, Missouri. AAH sent the three most promising fighters in the group—myself, George Fa'avae, and

Charles Martin—who weren't currently competing in the Olympic trials in Mobile, Alabama. The program wouldn't pay for PR's registration, flight, or hotel, but they gave him the time off to go compete. When John Bray, one of the coaches accompanying us, heard this, Bray offered to let him stay in his room.

On the first morning of the tournament, I was up early to grab a hotel breakfast when I noticed Coach Bray had beat me to the buffet. I sat beside him and immediately noticed how disoriented and disheveled he looked.

"Hey, Coach, you OK?"

"Fuckin' PR, man . . ." Bray replied, shaking his head.

"What about him? What happened?"

"Fuckin' guy was bangin' some chick in the room all night . . ."

I couldn't believe what he had just said to me. I didn't think Coach Bray was lying, but it's not like we were staying in suites. All the hotel rooms were set up in the typical style of two queen-sized beds in one room. This also meant PR had been out chasing girls the night before the fight he had paid to travel to and register in.

"That's wild, man. Wow."

That was the only response I could muster. John took a sip of his coffee and then returned to his room to try to get some rest before the tournament kicked off that afternoon. A few minutes later, PR showed up in the breakfast lobby and sat across from me before getting any food.

"Hey, what's up, Ed?"

"Nothing much, man. Just enjoying breakfast before the fighting starts this afternoon."

"Cool, cool. You see anyone else this morning?"

"Just Coach Bray, that's all."

PR let out a nervous laugh. "Oh yeah? He say anything about me?"

"Nah, why?" I shook my head in disappointment. PR's response made me certain that Coach Bray was telling the truth.

"Just wonderin', man. You know I snore like crazy. I thought Bray mighta said something about it." PR laughed, looking at me to see if I bought the story.

I didn't even bother looking at him and kept eating. "Nah, you good. He ain't say shit to me. Imma go rest a little more and start getting ready. Peace, brotha."

I left PR downstairs and spent the rest of the morning preparing for the tournament. I took the tournament seriously because I knew that if I lost, I was on my way home. Whatever happened with PR and Coach Bray had nothing to do with me, but it was an entertaining story to hear over my morning coffee.

I won my first two fights decisively, but I got my ass handed to me in the final by Cam Awesome. Cam holds the record for the most amateur national championships won at heavyweight, with five U.S. men's titles and four Golden Gloves titles. He won the national Golden Gloves tournament where I beat Dominic Breazeale by soundly defeating Donovan Dennis, the fighter who knocked me out of the tournament. No one expected me to get hurt fighting Cam, but no one expected me to win either—except me.

Regardless of how much better the opponent is, a fighter does himself no favors by mentally giving up before the fight. I thought I would pull off a fantastic upset and rock the amateur boxing world, but instead, Cam wiped the floor with me by a score of 33–10. Put another way, I only hit him ten times, while he hit me cleanly thirty-three times.

When we returned to AAH headquarters, I expected to be cut for losing. Instead, I was promoted because, en route to taking second place to Cam in the final fight of the tournament, I beat a fellow fighter in the program, Charles Martin. PR, meanwhile, was kicked out of the program for turning John Bray's hotel room into a brothel.

"Fuckin' Bray snitched on me, man; I'm out," PR said as he was packing his stuff.

"Snitched? For what?"

PR caught himself. "I mean, he made some shit up about me bringing a girl to the room."

"So you didn't do that?"

PR never answered me. He brushed the question off before selling me a knock-off Gucci coat and Polo Ralph Lauren shirt so he could have a little money. AAH had also cut him without paying him, as they considered the issue a conduct violation.

With PR gone, for the first time in my life, I found myself living alone. This allowed me to discover psychological strengths and weaknesses I never knew I had.

If You Do What Everyone Else Is Doing, You'll End Up Just Like Them

To make the most of my situation in California, I did a few things differently than the other boxers in the program. The gym where we trained was one mile from the apartment complex where all the boxers stayed. Every boxer drove themselves between the gym and the complex or took a shuttle. I figured this commute was a great way to get extra cardio training, so I ran there before practice, after we'd done our running for the day, and ran back at the end of our four hours of training and weight lifting.

After a few weeks, I noticed that the boxing gym was open in the evening for the neighborhood. So, I'd often go over in the evening and do extra training. I'd work on my shadowboxing and hit the heavy bag to continue improving my technique. That meant running another two miles, so on days when my legs needed to rest, I went to an LA Fitness across the street.

The LA Fitness was a five-minute walk away from my apartment. One afternoon, when my cell phone and iPod were dead, I left them in my apartment to charge. I'd normally be looking down, distracted by my electronic devices, but instead, I was looking straight ahead when a car lost control as it turned the corner and came up on the sidewalk. Because I was looking up, I jumped out of the way and escaped with only a few scrapes on my leg.

I was back in the gym the next day, but now I had a nagging feeling. I felt like I had just missed serious injury—or death—only because my electronics weren't charged. If I'd had them, I wouldn't have been able to react quickly enough. I felt blessed, but it was also the first time I realized boxing could be taken away from me, and I had no fallback plan or method to support myself. I only knew that when boxing was over, I didn't want to end up in what I call "the Fighter's Graveyard."

The Fighter's Graveyard is where boxers go when their career is on its final leg. It starts with taking fights where a guy is almost guaranteed to lose, but because he's got a decent record, the promoters can market the fight as a competitive match. However, everyone knows that the fighter's best days are behind him. The developing fighter gets another win on his record, and the has-been gets a payday, prolonging his acceptance of the end. From there, residents of the graveyard are relegated to coaching private clients, working in a gym, or, if they're not too physically beat up from their careers, some type of manual labor. Boxing has a steep opportunity cost. Also, it's not like other sports, where the athlete has made a lot of money along with accessing a pension plan and collecting a college degree. There isn't much else for most boxers after boxing ends.

I didn't want to be most boxers. To get ahead of what felt like an inevitable future, I started studying math before bed—all while downing my nightly box of wine. The irony wasn't lost on me. In any event, I was fascinated by math, but it had always been my weakest subject. In high school, I had either failed or barely scraped by in my math classes, and I failed calculus three times at community college before finally giving up. Still, I figured that if my plan to make millions as a boxer didn't work out, I'd need a fallback—and all the high-paying jobs I found required math.

I decided to figure out exactly why math gave me so much trouble. To do this, I thought back to when I first started having trouble with math. That took me back to the ninth-grade geometry class I'd passed, but only with a mighty struggle. Since geometry was so difficult, and knowing that each math discipline builds on those that came before, I thought back to the last math class that I really understood. I remembered I'd had difficulty dealing with inequalities, a concept you cover at the tail end of arithmetic and pre-algebra. Even working with fractions and decimals gave me trouble. By tracing my education backward in this way, I made a startling and instructive realization: I'd never properly learned the basics of math.

I started watching lessons a few evenings per week and doing problem sets in basic arithmetic and algebra. I approached math the same way I approached boxing: If I could take myself from a clumsy brawler who tripped over his feet to the level of a state champion who earned a sponsorship, I figured I should be able to pick up math. I thought, *If I could do this with my body, then I should be able to do this with my mind.*

From my boxing training, I now had a general model for learning and skill development. My success in boxing so far had not come from any talent or outstanding athleticism. It was earned through diligent practice and dedication, and I saw no reason why the same wouldn't work for math. In the same way that Chris Williams had worked with me on basic footwork and movement, I started relearning how fractions and the number line worked.

Between training and studying math, I was content and focused. I didn't socialize much, though. I didn't know anyone in the city, and with my driver's license suspended, meeting people or building a social life was nearly impossible. Relying on public transportation in Los Angeles is a social death sentence. I occasionally hung out with the guys in the program, but that was mostly driven by boredom. Outside of training, I didn't spend much time with people. This left room for my relationship with alcohol to grow even stronger.

An Addict by Himself Is in Bad Company

Loneliness leads to depression. I missed all the good times back home getting drunk with my friends. I didn't even have strangers to get drunk with, as the nearest bar was a twenty-five-minute walk away and in a relatively dangerous part of my neighborhood— in the three months I'd lived in LA, two shootings had occurred there. It was much easier just to grab a box of wine, a few 40s, or a bottle of liquor and drink at home.

One Saturday afternoon, I was feeling more isolated than usual. I was playing *Civilization* on the internet with friends back home. Although everyone was playing on their own computer, most of them were in the same room, and all of them were in the same city. I was playing with everyone and playing by myself, all at the same time. The sharp contrast of digital socializing and physical isolation sent me over the edge.

This marked the first time I consciously used alcohol to numb myself to negative emotions I was feeling—and I did it alone. I drank when I was excited, but that was when I was in a positive state of mind and celebrating with other people. Even when I drank alone at the bar, I wasn't technically alone. I could always spark up a conversation with the bartender to make myself feel like less of an alcoholic.

Getting drunk alone is a classic sign of alcoholism, and I knew it. I just didn't care. Despite the growing success of my boxing career and finally achieving financial stability, I was miserable—and drinking was the only thing that helped me forget that. Once I started drinking to numb my pain, I set myself on a path that never ends well and only gets harder the further down it you go.

From then on, a typical day in Los Angeles went like this: I'd wake up, go for a four-mile run, train boxing for four hours, then hit the weights. Afterward, I'd walk over to the Target by my apartment to buy a bottle of liquor, a box of wine, or both. And then I'd drink the evening away by myself, watching television or playing chess.

Drinking in Los Angeles was easy because I could walk into any grocery store or gas station and get alcohol. This was different from how things operated back home. In Pennsylvania, liquor sales are controlled by the state, so only certain stores can carry liquor. Currently, beer and wine are more freely sold in places, but in the early 2010s, you couldn't buy alcohol at commercial retailers in Pennsylvania. Living in California made it easier to drink whatever I wanted, wherever I wanted.

If I wasn't an alcoholic before moving to the West Coast, I became one while out there. I was crushing my morning runs and beating fighters while hungover and exhausted. Because I lived alone, as long as my performance didn't suffer, no one knew I was in a near-constant state of inebriation. My motivation to keep my drinking hidden made me train even harder, so that no one would question my ability.

One day, I barely made it to the scheduled pickup for the

shuttle to the park because I had gotten blackout drunk the night before.

"Damn, brotha, you smell like one of them homeless dudes down on Venice Beach," one of the other fighters said. "You good?"

"Shit, I'm here, ain't I?" I replied as I moved to the back of the van to pass out on the thirty-minute ride from Carson up to Burbank for the run through Griffith Park. "Just partied last night. I'm good, though."

"Ha, yeah, whatever you say, man. I swear I'm getting tipsy just smelling you," he replied. I had barely made it to the van, let alone had time to shower.

After those remarks, I had to beat them all running to prove that I was fine. It was a six-mile run through the hilly terrain of Griffith Park. I finished first by a huge margin because, if I didn't, I felt like word would get back to the decision makers at AAH that I cared more about drinking than I did about training.

Based on my behavior, that wouldn't be an incorrect conclusion. I knew there was a tough run scheduled for the next morning and got wasted again that night anyway. After my performance on that run, I slept for twenty hours, but no one asked any questions about my drinking.

It's surprisingly easy to become an alcoholic. Drinking triggers a massive dopamine release in the brain. Dopamine drives feelings of pleasure, motivation, and reward. So, alcohol gave me an artificial sense of happiness despite my loneliness and depression. The problem is that, over time, heavy alcohol use overwhelms the brain's dopamine receptors. It's like hitting a gong repeatedly— eventually, you stop hearing it. To keep feeling pleasure, alcoholics need more and more drinking to provoke the same dopamine effect.

This spiral was dangerous for me because drinking had become so entangled with my social life and sense of well-being. Without alcohol, I was even more isolated and unhappy, which drove me to drink more. It was a vicious cycle—loneliness drove drinking, and excessive drinking made it harder to feel genuine happiness or connection while sober. But in the moment, numbing my pain was all I could focus on, whatever the cost. Addiction is often driven by desperation to fill a psychological void, regardless of the harm it causes.

There are two types of alcoholics: those with a daily drinking dependence, and binge drinkers who lose control when they drink, even if they don't drink often. The first group understands they have a problem, as does everyone around them. Alcohol dominates their lives, and they feel physical withdrawal without it. Their compulsion to drink seems unfathomable to most.

I started as the latter, a binge drinker. I didn't need alcohol daily, but whenever I did drink, it brought out the worst in me. I couldn't stop at just one. For all-or-nothing personalities like me, moderation isn't possible. This type of alcoholic tends to fly under the radar. In your early twenties, binge drinking is celebrated. People who can party hard and hold ridiculous amounts of liquor are revered; those who can't keep up get ridiculed as being "lightweights."

I embraced the identity of champion drinker, chasing extremes to cement my status as a drinking legend. I mistook admiration of my drinking ability for actual liking and acceptance of me. In reality, binge drinkers have just as serious a problem as daily drinkers, but the heavy praise and enablement we receive early on only encourages our unhealthy relationship with alcohol.

Now, I no longer had that praise. I went to Los Angeles as a binge drinker who let things go too far, but I left a stone-cold alcoholic. For the remainder of my time in Los Angeles, I drank every day, and it was easy to hide because I lived alone.

Just Because Someone Is Your Opponent Does Not Mean They're Your Enemy

Cam Awesome was a problem for the AAH. To illustrate why, let's start with something Coach Yankello always said: "I can teach you how to fight, but I can't make you a fighter." The idea is that a coach can only teach you the technicals of a craft, but fighting requires more than just the knowledge of how to throw punches. There is an artistry in boxing that can't be taught.

Cam was like a painter who knew nothing about color, lighting, or texture—and he didn't want to learn. Cam cared about winning trophies but didn't care too much about how he did it. He didn't care about knocking a guy out, imposing his will on the other guy, or even boxing well. He cared about winning, and he discovered that the best way to do that was to accumulate more points than your opponent.

If this sounds simple, it is. Amateur boxing matches are scored based on who landed more clean hits. Compare this to professional boxing, where other factors are considered when judging a round: Cleanly landed punches still matter, but they are weighed against other markers such as punch activity, damage caused, ring general-ship, and defensive responsibility.

In 2015, the amateur system finally adopted the "ten-point must" scoring system—so named because in each round, one of the fighters has to receive ten points, while the loser gets nine or fewer—used in the professional ranks. But before amateur boxing switched to the ten-point must system, Cam had adapted his box-ing style to take advantage of the old scoring system. This meant that he focused on delivering as many punches as possible. He wasn't trying to knock his opponents out; he was just trying to score as many points as he could. Once he built up a sizable lead, he did anything to maintain it. That meant refusing to engage, holding opponents until the referee separated and reset them, or even dragging his opponent to the canvas during the clinch.

A major part of AAH's goal was to get a fighter to the Olym-pics. Cam stood in their way—and the way of every other would-be super heavyweight Olympic contender in the United States. He had no desire to turn pro, so waiting for him to leave wasn't an option. Guys refused to adapt to his style and train to beat it, as no one else was fighting like this at the next level. Professionals couldn't fight in his style and win, and since every boxer fighting amateur hoped to turn pro, most just accepted that losing to Cam was a necessary risk. While making it to the Olympics was a nice accomplishment to have on your résumé, you didn't need it to have a successful professional career.

Cam was an obstacle—and an expensive one, at that. If AAH failed to produce an Olympian, the program could be considered a failure, and all the money and time invested would have been wasted.

AAH initially flew Cam out to fight Jonathan Hamm, a six-foot-seven former tight end the program picked up after he was cut from NFL training camps and who was the 2011 national U.S. men's boxing champion. Their plan was to collect more film on Cam's fighting style and somehow unlock the secret to defeating him.

When they flew him out to fight Hamm, Cam stayed at my apartment. We went out for drinks and got along well. Cam didn't mind drinking the night before a fight, and I was just happy not to be drinking alone. The first time I had met Cam was in Kansas City, a few months earlier, when he handed me a one-sided beating. Meeting him this time, without the pressure of a fight and the bad intentions of trying to hurt and embarrass each other, was relaxing and a good time. I learned that he had gotten into boxing because he was tired of being bullied and that he didn't really care about it. He just enjoyed that it allowed him to see the world.

Cam went on to win his fight and then disappeared back to Kansas. Before he left, we swapped numbers to keep in touch. I returned to my evening routine of drinking and studying math.

If You Can't Do It Twice, You Got Lucky

One of the best parts about AAH was that they had the budget to keep all of their fighters fighting. The program put on USA-sanctioned boxing shows twice monthly. Either we fought each other, or fighters were flown in from around the country.

American amateur boxers can have a tough time getting fights because there simply aren't enough fighters in their region and weight class. Tournaments are held in different cities around the country, and most fighters can't afford to attend all of them. However, during my time at AAH, I fought in every tournament that I could because they sent me there. Before going to AAH, I'd had twenty-four fights in three years. Within nine months of joining AAH, I doubled that.

On October 2, 2011, Charles Martin and I traveled to Toledo, Ohio, to fight in the National PAL tournament. I had a chance to win a national boxing title and took it seriously, but I couldn't help myself when I discovered a cheap dive bar around the corner from the hotel. I wasn't going to drink in the hotel lobby, as I was worried about my coaches seeing me drink; if I lost, that would surely cause the program to cut me. But I still drank every night of the tournament, including the night before my most important fight.

Charles and I got paired again, in a rematch of our fight a few months earlier at the Ringside national tournament. This time, Charles was a better fighter than before and carried a chip on his shoulder about my promotion coming from his defeat. His loss to me in Kansas City hadn't caused him to get demoted, but I'm sure he came into our fight in Toledo feeling the pressure. For months, we had watched fighters get cut from the program after losing, so, from his perspective, if he lost to me a second time, he was going back to his life before AAH—a life that had included selling drugs, violence, and a few short stints in prison.

I didn't want to go home either. It was not lost on me how fortunate my situation with AAH was. I was making a decent amount of money while improving my boxing abilities. My experience of nearly getting run over had got me thinking that I didn't have a plan outside of boxing. For me, AAH was my ticket to freedom and my safety net from poverty. For both of us, this fight was the difference between a bright future or a return to a grim reality.

Charles did a better job keeping me away with his jab, but it's not like I hadn't improved since our last fight as well. I was able to step off and counter his shots easily, as my strategy for this fight was to make myself small and tight, forcing Charles to lean his six-foot-five frame past his center of balance to try to attack me.

Since my fight with Dominic Breazeale in the national Golden Gloves tournament, I'd only been in fights with guys taller and bigger than me, and I had learned that making myself smaller, in a crouched posture, made the fight easier for me, as it disguised my attacks and made it possible for me to execute surprise counterattacks. It forced my taller opponents to crouch over to find me, leaving them off-balance.

I also learned how to jab against taller opponents by studying the film of Mike Tyson. Tyson is most known for his knockout power, but he was an excellent boxer who made up for his short stature in the heavyweight division by using his jab. Later, when I was going over the tape with my coach, it was obvious that while Charles was hitting me, my jabs looked more impactful because they got through more cleanly, and many were vicious counterattacks.

I won the fight 14–12. It was a small margin of victory but still a victory. I beat the next guy in the tournament with a third-round stoppage, earning me a National PAL boxing title. This win ranked me as the number-four amateur heavyweight boxer in the United States and earned me a much-needed vacation. I might have been a full-blown alcoholic by this point, but as long as I kept winning, I could keep avoiding the truth.

Now, though, I had the chance for the real prize—the tournament to earn a spot on the 2012 men's Olympic boxing team.

VIII

Nothing Lasts Forever

The road to Olympic boxing starts with national qualifiers. The winners and second-place finishers of the big tournaments in the year of an Olympics get invited to a double-elimination tournament, and the winners of this tournament in each weight class become part of the United States Olympic team. They are then sent to the continental qualification tournament. There are five zones for the continental qualifier—Europe, the Americas, Africa, Asia, and Oceania. Under this format, someone can make the Olympic team but still not compete in the games. To compete in the games, you must finish in the top two or three at the continental qualification tournament.

By January 2012, the AAH program had been whittled down to five fighters: Charles Martin, Jonathan Hamm, Dominic

Breazeale, George Fa'avae, and me. AAH decided that we had the best shot of making it to the Olympic games; after that, they would promote our professional careers.

The 2012 men's national tournament, aka the Olympic trials, started on February 28, 2012. The tournament was held in Fort Carson, Colorado, six thousand miles above sea level, during a harsh winter. Physical activity would be challenging at that elevation, so AAH sent us up there two weeks before the fight to start training. This gave us an advantage over the other fighters who could not afford to arrive and train at elevation for weeks ahead of time.

Three days before the tournament started, I came down with a vicious flu. I had a pounding headache, chills, fatigue, and a fever of 102. The illness couldn't have come at a worse time. To make matters worse, the Olympic committee required each fighter to submit a urine sample after each bout. I could overcome the fatigue with coffee and the fever and chills with Tylenol, but I had no recourse for the real problem—the nasal and sinus congestion that made it impossible to breathe easily.

The World Anti-Doping Agency bans pseudoephedrine, the active ingredient in many decongestants, from competition, so I couldn't take that. I also didn't want to risk cross-contamination, so I avoided any other medication. I only used cough drops and Vicks, which did nothing.

I've fought through illness and injury before, and while it's not fun, it's also merely adding one more unpleasant feature to an experience that is already painful and unpleasant. No one at the tournament knew that I was sick. If I were matched against them,

I could strike fast and early and gain their respect, keeping them from being overly aggressive and slowing down the fight, so that I could keep up even in my weakened state.

I also felt I was better than the other fighters at AAH who came up with me—much better than some, while only marginally better than others. Still, I felt like I could beat anyone at that tournament, and the longer I lasted, the more I could expect my condition to improve. All I needed was an easy pairing in the first round, someone I was much better than who didn't know I was sick.

Fate disagreed. I was matched to fight Dominic in the first round. He now had a chance to avenge his loss to me a year earlier, and if he could pull it off, he'd crush my hopes of making the Olympic team.

Above All Things, Health. Without It, Nothing Is Possible.

Dominic had come a long way since our initial meeting one year before. The biggest difference was that he no longer let me cover distance so easily. In our first fight, I could push him around with pressure punches to the body, as he didn't understand how to make minute adjustments to keep me in his optimal punching range and me out of mine.

This time, he took quick shuffle steps backward while peppering me with his jab, forcing me to expend a lot of energy trying to press him into a corner. Still, I was faster and used to taller guys employing similar tactics, so at the end of the round, I was up 4–1. However, this was the hardest three-point advantage I'd ever fought for. With a stuffy nose, congested chest, and heavy fatigue, that three-minute round felt like I had just run a one-mile sprint. The one-minute rest between rounds felt like it lasted only a second.

The second round involved more of the same tactics: me pressing like a charging bull and Dominic moving around like a skillful matador. The difference was that this time, I was completely drained. Dominic could sense my waning energy levels and began engaging me with uppercuts when I took even a second to catch my breath and try to regain some energy. At full strength, a close engagement favored me and my fighting style. In my sickened state, I couldn't fight at the intensity required to make that style work.

When the bell sounded, I dragged myself back to the corner.

"You look like shit and are fighting worse. You good to keep going?" Jamal Abdullah was my coach. We'd been working together for a few months now, and he always kept it real with me. He knew what I was capable of, and he also knew how sick I had been the past few days.

"Yeah, man, I'm good," I responded. I was lying, but a fighter is never supposed to admit when he feels he can't continue—even when it's obvious that he can't. We leave that call up to the referee or our coach. Our mindset is always, "Come back with your shield or on it."

"Are you sure? Everyone knows you're sick. Ain't no shame in dropping this if you can't continue," he said, squirting ice-cold water down my throat. I tried to catch my breath mid-drink and choked. Normally, it would have been a light cough, but the illness made it sound like I was dying of lung cancer.

I wasn't worried about losing the fight. Losses no longer scared me because, of the five remaining fighters in the program, only one of us could win the tournament—assuming one of us won and not someone else. They weren't going to cut us all, as the plan was for us to start our professional careers after the tournament.

My real concern was going back to fight the third round. If I was too tired or unaware, I could take a shot that caused me serious damage. Life-changing shots were rare in the amateurs, but if I was going to take a shot that would affect me for the rest of my life, it would most likely be from a six-foot-seven, 250-pound heavyweight boxer while I was battling the flu.

"Call it. I'm done." I felt like a coward, but I knew it was the right thing to do.

I've never been afraid of getting hurt. You can't compete in something like boxing if you're worried about your personal safety. But that doesn't mean that you should be reckless. I couldn't expect Dominic to take it easy on me because I was sick. If I went out there in the third round, he should try to kill me. I had signed up for fighting knowing the risks, so if I went back out there in a state where I couldn't manage them, then I was going to lose anyway. The only difference would be that I might get carried out of the ring on a stretcher.

A corner retirement or corner stoppage—abbreviated "RTD [retired]" by BoxRec—is a term used in boxing to describe a fight that ends when, during any rest period between rounds, a boxer refuses to continue, or their corner pulls them out, thereby forcing the referee to call an end to the fight. This isn't the most dignified way to lose a match, but I could not keep fighting—especially against someone with Dominic's size and skill who knew of my compromised condition.

Dominic won our fight "referee stops contest—rd. 3" and went on to win the tournament and become part of the 2012 Olympic boxing team. I don't know if I would have won the tournament or even beaten him had I not been sick, but my illness played a role in the outcome. When Dominic and I first fought in April 2011, I was ready to take advantage of the opportunity. A year later, Dominic avenged his loss to me at the time when it mattered most.

Are You Hurt or Are You Injured?

We flew back to Los Angeles and hit the ground running. AAH managed to convince USA Boxing to hold the training camp for the continental qualification tournament at our gym. Dominic also needed a steady dose of sparring to get ready. All of us kept training, preparing for whatever came next, whether that was another amateur fight or our first professional bout.

While sparring with Charles Martin during this time, I got smashed with a snappy jab. There was nothing special about the way he'd thrown the punch, except that he took a little force off it, anticipating that I'd slip out of the way, as I had in hundreds of the previous rounds that we had sparred and the two matches we'd fought against each other. That day, either he was a little quicker than usual, or I was slightly more sluggish from nursing a hangover, because he hit me perfectly in the eye.

It stung a little more than usual, but at first, it didn't seem like any cause for alarm. I'd been hit by harder, more painful shots several times in my career. Pain and boxing are inexorably linked. When you block a punch, you still feel it in your arms or shoulders. Every punch that makes contact with the body, whether a clean shot to the ribs or a power shot parried, is unpleasant. But this unpleasantness is a part of the sport, and any fighter who can't take it won't last long.

We sparred five more rounds, each taking our share of clean and blocked punches, then called it a day. Afterward, my face was a little swollen, but nothing was unusual. The next day, my eye still hurt, but I thought nothing of it. Lingering aches the day after sparring were typical, especially when you did six rounds with a six-foot-five, 250-pound heavyweight with power in both hands.

Two days later, while I was sparring against another fighter in camp, we got into a clinch. In a clinch, one fighter holds the other, sometimes to frustrate him and other times to buy himself time to recover from the effects of a painful shot or equilibrium-disrupting punch.

I was applying pressure and keeping the fight close, as has always been my strategy as a shorter heavyweight. To gain separation to land a punch against my ribs, my opponent violently butted his shoulder into my head, making direct contact with the eye that Charles Martin had hit with the jab two days earlier. The pain was so intense that I immediately dropped to my knees.

I'd only taken a knee once before in a sparring session. That time, I had thought it would be a good idea to spar the night after heavy drinking, while my body was still flushing out the alcohol. My sparring partner had slipped my punch and launched a heat-seeking missile of a hook into my already overworked liver. Not only did I take a knee, I writhed around on the canvas in pain for five minutes in spectacular fashion. I wasn't as dramatic this time, but I knew something was wrong.

That afternoon, a CT scan revealed that the light punch Charles Martin landed forty-eight hours earlier had caused a blowout fracture. The shoulder shrug blew it wide open.

A blowout fracture occurs when an injury causes one of the delicate bones surrounding the eye to break. These orbital bones form a compartment, similar to a box, with the thinnest sections being on the inner side by the nose and on the floor below the eye. When blunt force trauma strikes the eye area, pressure transmits to the fragile orbital bones, which may then buckle or fracture from the impact. This "blowout" fracture releases pressure that could otherwise severely damage the eye itself. However, it can also entrap soft tissue in the break, cutting off the blood supply and eventually killing the eye tissues.

At first, I thought I'd just been hurt. But it turned out I'd been injured—and this injury not only required immediate surgery but also meant that I wouldn't be able to train for eight weeks or compete for twelve.

It's important to recognize the difference between being hurt and being injured. Being hurt is a normal part of boxing: You get hurt every day, and part of your job is to fight your way through it.

But when you're injured, you need to recognize that and take the time to recover. If you don't, and you try to push on, then you risk making it worse, which can have long-term repercussions.

The Only Thing Worse Than Not Making a Deal Is Making a Bad One

"So can I still drink?" That was the first question I asked after they told me I'd need surgery and twelve weeks to fully recover.

"Umm, sure," the doctor said. "Just don't do anything under the influence that could affect your eye."

"All right then. No problem."

For the first two weeks after surgery, I couldn't do anything but rest. I couldn't even let my heart rate get too high, as the change in blood pressure could affect the healing of my eye socket. For six weeks after that, I could only do nonimpact workouts. This meant I couldn't run or hit the heavy bag, and sparring was definitely out of the question. However, I could ride the exercise bike and shadowbox. So, for the next six weeks, I divided my time between them.

Reduced training also meant that I could drink a lot more without worrying whether a hangover would affect my performance. During my recovery, I discovered that fortified wine, more colloquially known as "bum wine," was available in California, and it was the perfect way to pass the time. Bum wines are cheap wines with sugar, artificial flavors, and artificial coloring added. Some versions taste great, while others taste and smell like the fruit is still in the middle of fermenting. They're the perfect choice for an alcoholic with high taste and a low budget; a fifth of MD 20/20—"Mad Dog"—was only six dollars. I'd cycle between MD 20/20, Thunderbird, Wild Irish Rose, Night Train, and Cisco. A market on the way to the gym sold all different types of bum wine, so it was easy to pick up a bottle on the way back from the gym.

In my attempts to control my drinking, I had given myself a rule: no hard liquor while drinking alone. Beer and malt liquor were easy to put down, but I'd have to drink way too much to get a proper buzz going. Regular wine was strong enough to get buzzed on, but it was expensive per volume. However, bum wine was just right. It was cheaper than wine, stronger than beer, and tasted great. Bum wines were my best friend during my recovery from my eye injury.

The final four weeks of my recovery cleared me for all impact activities except sparring. This meant I could return to my mile-long runs and start hitting the bag. Around this time, AAH approached me with a professional promotional contract to look over. I'd never seen a professional boxing contract, but some things immediately caused alarm.

First, there was the amount of money they were planning to pay me. Now, I've always known that there isn't much money to make in professional boxing. Whenever you see a superstar on TV, know that he is the exception and that most boxers are not making millions. They usually have a second job.

Therefore, I wasn't surprised when the contract said they would start by paying me only a thousand dollars per round. But

I found it odd that this payment would replace the stipend and the rent for the apartment. Although most boxers don't receive meals, housing, and a four-thousand-dollar monthly salary, the same program that had given me those things for the past fourteen months was now expecting me to stay with them and take less money.

Despite these downsides, I still saw the value of turning pro with a promotional contract, because that meant I wouldn't have to worry about selling enough tickets to cover what it cost for me to fight. Fighters who don't have promoters can only fight if they sell enough tickets to cover the opponent's costs, including his purse, travel, and lodging. If you can't sell enough tickets to cover opponents and don't have a promoter, you'll be forced to take fights where you have zero chance of winning and are only being used to develop another fighter. So I could still reason to myself that being forced to earn my living on prize money alone was a reasonable, albeit unexpected, standard—especially when weighed against the opportunity of starting my professional career with a boxing promoter. It was the final condition that I couldn't wrap my head around.

AAH expected me to live and train in Los Angeles. This was not standard in the boxing industry, and it would introduce heavy financial responsibility and force me to live and fight desperately. Generally, fighters lived wherever they wanted to, as promoters picked boxers from all over the country. Part of the reason I could deal with the changes to the payment structure was that I figured I'd just move back to Pittsburgh, a city with a much lower cost of living than Los Angeles. But AAH was not on board with my plan.

Those conditions made signing with AAH impossible. Of

course, I also knew that the moment I told them I wouldn't sign with them, they'd take that as me quitting the program. So, I knew that AAH and I would be parting ways at this point, but I couldn't voluntarily leave. They had to let me go; it was the only way I could qualify for unemployment benefits.

I knew that no matter what happened, AAH couldn't get rid of me in the next four weeks. It's against the law to fire an employee because of an injury suffered at work. I was safe until the doctor gave me the all-clear to return to full contact.

I spent the next three weeks mostly drinking. I was still bored and lonely, and on top of that, I now had an added point of stress. I had used my money to pay off debt, to build my credit, and, now that I had gotten my license back, to get a car, but I didn't have anything saved, and I still had no plan for the future other than to fight.

Leverage Is Everything, but Nothing Is Guaranteed

On May 12, 2012, Dominic Breazeale defeated Ytalo Perea at the continental qualifying tournament in Rio de Janeiro, earning him a spot at the 2012 London Olympics. This was the beginning of the end of AAH.

When Dominic made the Olympic team, he was courted with different offers from established boxing promoters. AAH expected Dominic to sign with them, as they had bankrolled his boxing career from his first amateur boxing match to his final amateur fight against the Russian Magomed Omarov in the preliminary rounds of the 2012 Olympics.

AAH's plan, from its inception, had been to build a heavyweight champion. The best way to achieve this was to develop a fighter as an amateur, as it had with Dominic. However, this left AAH exposed to the possibility of their resources and money being wasted. Amateur fighters are not allowed to sign a promotional contract, which causes them to lose their amateur status. This meant that for AAH to work, the program had to operate in good faith that a fighter would return the favor and stick with them if they got to the Olympics.

The program had creatively sidestepped the issue of promotional contracts, as the stipend and housing its fighters received were considered sponsorships, and we were paid like employees. We didn't receive money to participate in a fight, so we weren't considered professionals. Every two weeks, two thousand dollars hit my bank account like I was a regular W-2 employee.

However, AAH apparently didn't consider that Dominic would have significant leverage once he made the Olympic team. Dominic became disgruntled with the program after they refused to fly his wife and children out to see him fight in London. This wasn't an unreasonable request and was far less than many other Olympic team members had received. AAH also offered considerably less money than other promoters despite having no experience promoting professional fights. Michael King believed that his previous success in television with King World Productions, and the fact that he and his investors had bankrolled Dominic's development, were adequate justifications for him to sign with them despite the drawbacks.

Dominic disagreed and ultimately signed with manager Al Haymon and Premier Boxing Champions (PBC). AAH was geared up to become a professional outlet, but all of the investors pulled out after Dominic left. The program didn't shut down immediately, but they started to viciously cut costs. Over the next few weeks, I watched the program fire its trainers, chefs, and coaches.

After they got rid of all the extras, I knew the fighters would be next. Despite my success, I was on the chopping block for two reasons: my size and persistence. Of the four remaining, I was the shortest and lightest. While I had proven that I could win against bigger guys, size is never a disadvantage. I couldn't get taller, and adding muscle would slow me down without increasing my punching power. The heavyweight division was dominated by guys who fit this profile, so my stock took a hit.

My persistence in changing the contract terms was also starting to annoy them. I was not willing to take a substantial pay cut, lose my housing, *and* be forced to remain in the fourth-most expensive city in the world. I didn't need them to change all of those points. Just one would have been enough—but they would not budge.

I would have probably been cut then and there if my eye injury wasn't protecting me. But I'd soon lose that insurance policy as well.

Sometimes the Best Thing to Happen to You Is Not Getting What You Want

My first fight back was against Cashton Young, from nearby Compton, California. He'd been coming to the gym and training faithfully with everyone because he hoped to get recruited by AAH. His dream wasn't impossible to achieve, as AAH had recruited fighters this way.

Cashton could hit hard, but he had nowhere near my experience, training, and athleticism. I imagine AAH matched me with him to make sure that I was fully healed before they cut me loose. He put up a good fight, swinging dangerous overhand rights, but I easily dealt with them and even managed to stun him a few times. The first round was close, but I took over after he realized his most powerful weapon was ineffective. I smothered his shots with pressure and used my strength and size to keep him pressed against the ropes—which is why everyone in attendance that afternoon was stunned when his arm was raised as the victor.

I'm never one to take a victory away from a fighter, but it's hard to see how I lost that fight. The only thing that made sense to me was that AAH wanted a way to cut their losses and cover their asses. If I were to get knocked out, they'd have to let me recover before cutting me. So, if I didn't knock him out, they'd ensure he won the fight.

This might sound like I'm making excuses, but remember—I didn't want to be there anymore. And it's not uncommon for in-house, hometown judges to become suspiciously incompetent when there is influence from the show's promoter.

"When you get finished cleaning up, can you come into my office?" Eric said. He was operations director of the program. If he wanted to talk to me, I knew it meant they had either finally budged on some of my contract terms, or I was getting the boot.

"Yeah, sure thing, man. Gimme a few more minutes." I should

have told him to just do it and be done with it, but I wanted to take in the locker room one last time. After giving everything one good look, I dragged myself to the office. I still held on to a sliver of hope that they had changed their minds, but I was realistic.

"Hey, Ed, have a seat," Eric said. He was soft-spoken, which is a good trait to have when you're going to fire someone. However, I didn't let my guard down.

"Man, this is it, ain't it? Y'all cuttin' me loose, right?"

"Looking at the future of the program, we've decided that we're gonna go in a different direction. It's nothing personal. You're a good fighter, but you're not what we think will give the program the best chance for success."

Why not just say *you're too small and stubborn*? I wanted to say that to him, but I didn't. It didn't matter why they were cutting me. They'd made up their minds. There was only one question to ask.

"So what about my pay for the rest of my time? How's that work?"

"Well, you have two options. We can pay you out for the remainder of the pay period, or you can take a prorated payment for days in this pay period that you were part of the program and apply for unemployment if you stay in the state."

A few weeks earlier, when I started disputing the contract terms, some of the guys had told me to take the unemployment option even if I wasn't going to stay in the state. It was always approved, and the whole system was online, so you could keep getting paid anywhere. I didn't know what would happen after I left

AAH, but I knew that it would cost money, and I didn't have a job laid out.

"Just prorate me," I said. "What's that work out to, anyway?"

"Five hundred sixty-two dollars." Eric already had the check prepared.

"And when do I have to be out of the apartment?"

"Three days."

Shit. They didn't play.

"Thanks, Eric." I got up to leave.

"Best of luck to you," he said, but I barely heard him—I was already out the door.

I wasn't surprised, and I had no hard feelings. The fifteen months that I spent in Los Angeles had taken my boxing abilities to a new level. In just over a year, I'd gone from an obscure amateur club fighter to a national champion and achieved a peak ranking of number four in my weight division by USA Boxing. The program's financial support had also allowed me to pay off some debt and get a car—a car that I would need to drive back home across the country to Pittsburgh.

This was a win for me. I could return home to Pittsburgh while still collecting unemployment from California. Now, I could reunite with Tom and continue my training under him.

I'd managed to pull myself out of the tailspin that had started after I quit football—I'd risen to the challenge that Dr. Roberts gave me. But I didn't realize at the time that this was only a superficial fix. Until I dealt with the underlying problems, I wasn't going anywhere.

IX

If Your Miserable Life Doesn't Motivate You, Nothing Will

At first, I was excited about taking a road trip across the United States. I thought about all the different sights I'd see and places I'd visit during my drive from LA to Pittsburgh. Then I looked at the reality of my situation, and the trip went from a leisurely excursion to potentially one of the most stressful things I'd ever do.

First, there were the financial limitations. Part of the deal that allowed me to file for unemployment was that my termination was effective immediately. Otherwise, they'd reject my unemployment claim. So, that meant I would be making the drive across the country with just the $562 check that Eric had cut me, having spent the rest of the money I'd earned before that on paying down my debt.

I found a website to calculate how much money I'd need for gas on the fastest route. In the summer of 2012, gas in Los Angeles was five dollars per gallon. The farther east I went, the cheaper gas became, but it would still cost me three hundred dollars; half of the money I had was already spent before I factored in any money for food or lodging. For an emergency, I had opened a secured credit card with five hundred dollars in credit, but that didn't give me much room for any issues that could potentially arise.

The only chance I had at making this trip within my budget was to take the fastest route possible that avoided tolls. Most of the route was along I-70 from Colorado Springs to Pennsylvania. A large swath of that highway cuts through Tornado Alley, which added another degree of stress to the trip; I'd seen videos of the fierce storms and tornados that would destroy anything in their path. I checked the weather, and it appeared that I'd have nothing but clear skies for the entirety of my road trip. This was a relief.

Staying at even the dingiest hotels was financially out of the question, so I asked friends at three points along the way if I could sleep there when I passed through the city. They all agreed, but the first stop was a twenty-four-hour drive away from LA, in Colorado Springs. So, somewhere along the way, in Nevada or Utah, I'd have to pull off the highway and sleep in my car.

I hit the road on August 30, 2012. The scenery for the first four hours of the trip was a barren desert, but once I got past Las Vegas, my surroundings became beautifully mountainous. The rugged terrain of Utah and Colorado was breathtaking. After Colorado Springs, though, the country quickly became boring and flat, and everything smelled like cow shit.

My next stop was in Kansas City, where Cam lived. I arrived in the evening and quickly went to sleep. The next morning, my car wouldn't start. I had it towed to a mechanic and learned that I needed a new fuel pump. The repair set me back $450—thank goodness for that credit card I had taken out. The repair took a week, and that added another degree of stress. I had hoped my unemployment payments would have started by the time I reached Kansas City, but that didn't happen. Now, I was in a race to get home before I ran out of money.

Time was also working against me. I had planned on making the trip in four days, but the car repairs and the stress made it a two-week affair that strained my body, emotions, and finances. And when I arrived, I learned that this was only the beginning of my troubles.

Help When You Can, but Always Let a Person Retain Their Dignity

Once I arrived in Pittsburgh, I would need a place to live. My unemployment benefits wouldn't be enough to cover a security deposit, let alone rent, anywhere—and that was assuming I still got them. If the unemployment office found out that I was no longer living in California, they'd cut them off. For now, I was using a friend's address to create the illusion of still being in California. My only plan was boxing, and that was a terrible plan. I wasn't even a professional earning money for fights yet.

The first place I went to was Matt and Bill's house. I arrived

Sunday morning, just in time for football. I picked up a case of beer right before I arrived so we could reunite in style. Before the game started, Matt made me an offer.

"So, Bill and I were thinking that you could stay here, in the extra room, for two hundred dollars a month?"

I was genuinely surprised. The brothers were two of my best friends, but I hadn't been expecting them to make this lifesaving offer.

"Oh yeah, that's great, man," I responded. "Because I had *no* idea what I was going to do."

"Awesome," Matt said. "Now, let's drink and watch football!"

Their parents owned the house they lived in. They paid rent to their parents as a gesture of respect, but they didn't need my money, even to cover the utilities I used. Still, charging me *something* let me hold on to my sense of self-respect in a way that would've been tough if they gave the room to me for free. If it wasn't for their help, I would've been in serious trouble.

The next day, I drove up to Tom's gym. The drive was way more relaxing without having to worry about getting pulled over.

"I'm ready to turn pro," I told Tom.

"Why the hell does everyone want to turn pro?" Tom said. "That shit is so stressful, and the money sucks."

"But there *is* money. And you coach pro fighters! What the hell?"

"Yeah, because what else am I gonna do? I've been doing this for twenty years. I don't know anything else. And I'm tellin' you, there ain't no rush."

"No rush? I'm twenty-seven!"

"Ah shit, you got time. Look at guys like Tarver or Stevenson—great fighters and champions. Guys don't even really start to understand boxing until they're in their thirties anyway. And you're heavyweight, so you got even more time to develop." Antonio Tarver and Adonis Stevenson had turned pro at twenty-eight and twenty-nine years old, respectively. I didn't see the big difference from twenty-seven but decided not to argue.

"You know this game better than I do," I told Tom. "Whatever you say, man. But I don't know how we're gonna get amateur fights. I ain't got the money or time to always travel out of town for fights."

On top of that, there were even fewer amateur heavyweights in the region than when I had left fifteen months ago. All of the guys I had fought had either turned pro or stopped fighting. There were some new guys, but they had just started, and there was no way their coach was going to let them fight me, an open-class, ranked fighter with over forty wins and a national title.

"We'll figure it out," Tom said. "Trust me. This is the best long-term play."

I trusted Tom's judgment and followed the plan. I won my first amateur fight back, although I had to drive forty minutes out for it. I could deal with that distance. My second amateur "fight" was scheduled a little farther out. It was still manageable, but that fight reminded me of all the reasons why I wanted to be done with the amateur system—and this time, my mind would be a lot harder to change.

Everyone Has a Breaking Point

In amateur boxing, it's not unheard of for a scheduled opponent to not show up. It's still frowned upon, but amateur club-level fighters often decide that the possibility of getting hurt or embarrassed is not worth the plastic trophy or dollar-store medal that they could win. Of course, they accept the fight and fool everyone, their coach included, into thinking that they're going to compete, but when it comes time to get checked by the doctor before the bout, the fighter is nowhere to be found, and their cell phone has mysteriously died.

As an amateur boxer, there were several occasions where I only found out that my opponent wasn't going to show up after I'd driven an hour to the location of the bout or after I'd waited through three hours and fifteen fights on a Saturday night, hoping that my opponent would show up, only to discover that his car "broke down."

In October 2012, I was supposed to fight a guy about an hour north of the city. I arrived at the venue, where his coach informed me that the fighter had lost his "passbook." Passbooks are the official record books of your wins and losses that you had to show to prove that you were in good standing with USA Boxing (the organization that oversees amateur boxing in the United States). Now the entire system is online, but in 2012, this was how they kept track of fighters.

The officials agreed to let him fight because he had just competed locally, so they knew he was up-to-date and didn't have any violations, sanctions, or suspensions. All he needed was a way to get to the fight. I got his number from his coach and got to work.

"Yo, it's Ed Latimore," I said when he picked up the phone. "We were supposed to fight tonight. What happened, fam?"

"Ah man, I can't find my passbook. You know how it is. They ain't gonna let me fight without it."

"Nah, bruh. They said if you can get here, you good."

"Shit. I ain't got a whip, though."

"It's all good. I'll drive and pick you up. Your coach said he'll drive you back."

"Really?"

"Yeah. You ain't scared, are you?"

"Ha ha, nigga, Imma fuck you up and talk shit the whole way there."

"Aight. Bet. See you in like ninety minutes."

I hit the road, exercising every shred of self-control to stay under the speed limit. If I got pulled over, we probably wouldn't make the fight in time. Thirty minutes into the drive, I got a call from his coach.

"Hey, Ed, man, don't even bother. The officials said they can't skirt the rules. They gotta do everything by the book."

"Shit! For real?"

"Yeah, man, I'm sorry."

"It's all good."

I so rarely get angry that when I do, my body physically hurts. That night, I was hurting. I was disappointed that I'd wasted my time and gas, and angry that I'd invited my friends to drive an hour to see a fight that wouldn't happen. When I got back to my city, I met up with some friends and began to drown my anger in whatever alcohol was available.

I knew I had to go pro. If I fought as a professional, there'd be money on the line, and that would make it less likely for guys to back out at the last minute. I couldn't keep investing my time, money, and energy into fights that only paid in experience, with the slim hope of reaching a tournament, where I'd have to cover the costs of travel, lodging, and registration myself. When I was with All-American Heavyweights, they had covered those expenses, sending me all over the country to fight. But now, I was on my own.

"Shit like this happens all the time in boxing—and it won't stop just because guys are getting paid," Tom said when I told him my plans. He was still trying to convince me to stay amateur.

"Yeah, but at least I'll get paid for my time," I said. "Right now, win or lose, I'm not getting any closer to the goal, whether they show or don't show."

"Your time ain't gonna be worth that much if you turn right now . . . but if you wanna turn now, all this talking ain't gonna help you get ready. Start workin'." That was Tom's way of giving up and getting on board with the plan.

Just Because You're a Pro Doesn't Mean That You're a Professional

Most people refer to boxing—along with mixed martial arts—as a "combat sport." The only thing it has in common with the "Big

Four"—basketball, football, hockey, and baseball—is that it's a physical competition. Aside from the competitors relying on their bodies to win and earn a living, boxing is a different animal.

Unlike other sports, in boxing, violence is how you keep score. Football is physical, but you don't get points for it—the goal is to get the ball in the end zone, not hit the other guy as hard as you can. There are also some limits to the violence. Even before football changed many rules to make it safer, there were still penalties for "holding," "unnecessary roughness," and "illegal hands to the face." You can't survive a boxing match without holding, being rough, and putting your hands in someone's face.

Fighting is technically allowed in hockey because the referee doesn't interfere until the guys are down on the ice or one player has such an advantage that he could seriously injure his opponent. But the player who instigates the fight is removed from play for five minutes. In boxing, the athlete who causes the most damage to his opponent is typically the winner. There's no penalty box or fouls for excessive force—only point deductions for blows to the groin or behind the head, and *only* if continued after multiple warnings. The goal is to hit your opponent as hard and as often as possible, ideally rendering them unconscious in the process. What would be considered assault in any other context is not just permitted in boxing—it's the very essence of the sport.

There is one other notable difference between combat sports and their less violent counterparts: the barrier to entry. In the Big Four sports, there's a developmental process. Players start playing when young, make their high school team, then compete for a starting spot. From there, they catch the attention of colleges or minor developmental professional leagues. It's "invite only," even if you want a tryout. From this point, a team selects you to be on their roster.

With combat sports, on the other hand, anyone can become a "professional athlete," assuming they pass the physical tests required to get a state and federal boxing license. Because anyone can join the professional party, there is no outside money or help when you start fighting. Many fighters go their entire career covering the full cost of their medical tests and training. When you factor in the other costs of being a fighter—gear, training, gym fees, and travel—most fighters start their career in the negative, spending more money than they make. Unless you turn pro as a highly touted amateur with multiple national championships, no one is footing the bill for your expenses. I had a decent amateur career that got me a national championship, and I even had a win over an Olympian on my résumé, but I was one of those fighters who had to finance my own career at the start.

If You Hate Your Life, Do Something About It—Because No One Else Will

My new job at T-Mobile paid $9.28 per hour, plus commission on phones and products sold. The wage put me in a position that many people are familiar with: I wanted as many hours as I could get while simultaneously looking for any reason to call off. The job wasn't bad, and I enjoyed the people I worked with, but I hated that I didn't have any other options in my life but to stand on my feet for eight hours a day to make so little money that I couldn't afford the product I was selling.

One cold November night, a customer entered the store at 8:58 p.m. While the store closed at 9:00 p.m., T-Mobile's policy was that employees couldn't kick anyone out at closing time, nor were we allowed to turn anyone away, regardless of how close to closing time they entered.

"Shit!" I mumbled to myself. I was hoping this person had wandered into the wrong building, but when they started to leisurely browse, I knew this was no mistake.

"Good evening! Is there anything I can help you find? Do you have any questions about anything?"

"Ah, yeah, I'm looking for a new phone. I'm way past the point for an upgrade. But I don't know the best phone I should get, so I figured I'd come into the store and ask a rep."

I'd always wondered how, in the e-commerce age, cell phone stores still managed to exist. Many people were ordering phones online, but working at T-Mobile had shown me that there was still a large number of people who preferred to shop the old-fashioned way. At least now I had a chance to make a sale and earn a little commission from this last-minute straggler.

"Well, let me show you some of the newest options we have!" I smiled and got back into salesman mode. I couldn't change the time or make the customer leave, so I embraced the situation and did my best to close the sale.

Salesmen get a bad rep, but that's only because people remember their negative experiences far more easily than their positive ones. Like with random cold calls with a friend you haven't seen in years, who's disguising a meet-up as a chance to pitch their multi-level marketing scheme, everyone has a bad memory of someone trying to sell them something. However, people forget that the majority of their sales experiences tend to be positive, ending with them getting what they want and being happy to have spent the money.

As a sales rep, making a significant part of my living on commission, I always remembered that if someone walked through the door, they were looking to spend money. In many cases, all I had to do was push them over the hump. I found that the best way to do this was by adopting a polite and friendly demeanor and never pushing too hard for the sale. This approach required patience.

Despite my facade of cordial calmness with my late-night customer, I was constantly checking the clock. By the time I explained every feature of every phone in the store, nearly an hour had passed.

"I think we've covered everything we have in the store. Do you have any more questions, or is there one you've got your heart set on?"

"Thank you so much. I feel a lot better about this. I'm going to come in tomorrow and pick up that Samsung Galaxy you showed me!"

"Excellent! Well, have a good night!"

"You too!"

"WHAT THE FUCK?!" I shouted after she left, alone in the store and frustrated. Not only had this woman caused me to stay an hour past closing time, she didn't even buy a phone. Worse, her plan to come in the next day to buy it meant that someone else would get the commission off *my* hard work and extra time investment.

I started emptying the day's register and balancing the sales, but I was so frustrated that I kept making basic math errors, forcing me to restart the process several times. Those mistakes added another hour to my closing routine. Usually, I would have activated the security system by nine-thirty and been on my way to drink. That night, I didn't leave the store until almost midnight.

I sat in my car when I got to it, stewing in a cauldron of negative emotions. I was angry, sad, disappointed, and frustrated. More than anything, I felt powerless. I was twenty-seven, with no skills to do anything but a customer-service job. I hated my job and hated that I needed it to survive.

I thought back to nearly getting run over in California and how it had motivated me to improve my math skills in the hopes of returning to college. I had been slacking on studying over my first two months at home; I was too busy training, working, and making up for lost drinking time with my friends. But that evening, I got a painful glimpse of what my future would look like if I had to stop boxing, and it reignited my commitment to giving myself more options.

In 2020, STEM (science, technology, engineering, and mathematics) workers had median wage and salary earnings of about sixty-four thousand dollars. That was much higher than the forty thousand earned by those working in non-STEM occupations, which is approximately twenty dollars an hour. I had seen this play out in my own life: When I was twenty-one, I worked as a

Starbucks barista. Most of my fellow coffee slingers at the store had bachelor's or master's degrees. None had majored in STEM.

I researched which jobs had the highest salaries and employee satisfaction. One thing became abundantly clear: If I wanted to go down this path and get an economically valuable degree, I'd have no choice but to fix my math skills. It couldn't just be something I did whenever I had some free time. All of the highest-paying, happiest jobs required a strong math background.

I resumed studying more intensely than before, taking any dead time at work to look up problems and study on my work computer. In Los Angeles, I had begun relearning math with the assumption that I barely understood arithmetic—simple addition, subtraction, multiplication, and division—and spent most of my time shoring up those deficiencies. I did the same thing with each successive level of math until I was confident that I understood it, allowing me to move on to the next level—whether it was calculus or any other math class I would need to get my degree. I had reached a level where I could do some simple calculus problems, but I still wasn't comfortable with it. If I was serious about going back to college, I needed to now approach calculus the way I had approached learning the basics, which I modeled after the way I had learned how to box: by moving through the four levels of competence.

I had another problem besides learning math: paying for school. If I wanted to go back, improve my résumé, and land a better-paying job, I needed to figure out how to afford it. But I wasn't ready to throw away the four years of hard work I'd put into boxing. After weeks of searching for a solution, I landed upon what I believed was my best chance at keeping my dreams alive: enlisting in the National Guard.

Nothing Goes According to Plan, So Plan Accordingly

The National Guard markets itself as a way to serve your country "one weekend a month and two weeks a year." It seemed like the perfect solution—I could keep boxing, go to school, and get the financial support I needed for my education. But the more I looked into it, the more I realized it wasn't quite that simple.

While it's true that the drilling for the National Guard is one weekend per month, plus a two-week training exercise, there's a good chance the army will deploy you at some point during your enlistment, which nullifies the reason many people enlist in the National Guard in the first place. Your enlistment in the National Guard also lasts eight years instead of four, and you undergo basic training, like any other military branch. That meant I'd have to be away for ten to thirty-three weeks, depending on my military occupational specialty (MOS).

Still, all of that was an easy trade-off for me. I didn't mind the possibility of being deployed and I didn't mind going away for basic training—especially since the army would pay me, and I'd have no living expenses. It'd be like returning to AAH, except I wouldn't be boxing. I'd be soldiering.

On January 4, 2013, I officially entered the United States Army National Guard. I also received an unexpected opportunity to test my new math skills when I enlisted. The army requires you to take the Armed Services Vocational Aptitude Battery (ASVAB), an exam that evaluates an enlistee across diverse areas, including arithmetic reasoning, math knowledge, and verbal skills. The resulting score provides an integrated snapshot of a recruit's analytical capabilities and specialized job-match potential within the armed forces.

I scored a 99, the highest score possible and one that less than 1 percent of ASVAB takers achieve. The math on the ASVAB covers everything taught before calculus, proving beyond the shadow of a doubt that I had successfully built my foundation. My nearly perfect score on this exam confirmed that my path to higher mathematics was right. At the very least, it validated that I had sufficiently filled the gaps in my knowledge.

This score allowed me to pick a MOS I wanted. I chose to become a 94A—a land combat electronic missile system repairer. For this occupation, after I completed my ten weeks of basic training, I'd go to advanced individual training (AIT) for twenty-eight weeks. While that was over half a year I'd spend away from boxing, it was time I planned on using to save up money, and it would be an investment in my future. I wanted to start right away, but that would not be possible.

"So, the next alignment for basic training and a starting class for your AIT means you can't start basic training until June 4," the army recruiter told me. "You'll leave the day before." I felt my stomach drop.

The unemployment benefits I was getting from California would run out before then. I needed those benefits to afford my car payment, training expenses—including the gas costs from driving sixty miles a day—and rent.

"Wait, what? That's five months away. How is that even possible?"

"Army's got a schedule for everything. If you wanna leave earlier, you're free to pick another MOS. Your score's high enough to do whatever job you want."

I considered his offer. Then, I remembered I wasn't enlisting just for the sake of adding it to my résumé. I had chosen the 94A MOS because of the skills I'd develop and the training I'd receive.

"Nah, that's all right. That gives me more time to tie up some loose ends before I take off." Running out of my employment benefits was a problem, but it wouldn't happen until the middle of March. I felt confident that I could figure out how to survive for the rest of my time before enlistment.

"That's the spirit," the recruiter said.

I knew that I'd have to put my boxing career on hold eventually. When I enlisted, I figured I'd start basic training before turning pro. Now that I wasn't leaving for another five months, though, I thought that I could get some professional fights in first, and maybe that would bridge the gap between my unemployment ending and starting with the National Guard.

I thought this was a great plan, but not everyone was thrilled with it.

There's No Such Thing as a Free Punch

"So, what, you're just gonna stop boxing?"

Tom was pissed when I told him my plan. He put a lot of time and energy into his fighters and saw my potential. Still, I had to do what was best for me and my future. This was no different than when I had started training with Tom one year ago. I had bet on myself then and done what was best for me. Now, I was making a similar bet.

"For a short while, yeah," I said.

"How the hell are you gonna fight and be in the army?"

"I don't leave until June. I'll get some fights, take off, and come back to it."

"Well, we got you an opponent for your pro debut: Jon Hill."

Hill was an interesting choice for my debut opponent. He was a six-foot-four, 250-pound southpaw with four wins; his only loss having come at the hands of Dan "the Mountain" Martz, who earned his ring name because he's built like a mountain and he used to work in the mines in West Virginia. At the same time, Hill's four wins had come against opponents with a combined record of 2–27.

One of the open secrets in boxing is that a fighter's record doesn't mean anything. To understand how good he is, you have to look at who he's fought and see videos of his previous fights. There wasn't any video of Hill online, so we only had reports on his ability from other coaches. Whatever information Tom had gotten made him confident in my ability to handle the fight, and so my training began.

Preparation for the fight wasn't the hard part. By now, I was used to the training grind. I knew what it was like to work eight hours a day standing on my feet and then head to the gym for four hours, only to wake up and do it all over again. The part that took me by surprise was the frustration of selling tickets.

A boxer's journey to stardom often begins in humble venues like converted fire halls and reception centers. These small-scale events, organized by local promoters, serve as proving grounds for fighters to gain experience before they're ready for the big stage. While these shows prioritize profitability over developing a fighter's reputation, they play a crucial role in a boxer's career progression. However, these fights are rarely streamed and never televised, limiting the exposure a fighter receives in their early professional bouts.

If a fighter wins enough at this lower level, he's then in a position to receive a contract from one of the major boxing promoters. This is the Holy Grail for an up-and-coming boxer, because without a major promoter, there's no way for a fighter to get the bigger televised fights and the paydays that come with them.

Let's say a network (Fox, ESPN, DAZN, etc.) shows twelve fights yearly. Promoters (PBC, Top Rank, Golden Boy Promotions, etc.) know that the networks have more money to put behind a fight. This is how their fighter gets publicity, so promoters compete for those dates to get their fighters on TV for more money and more exposure. Fighters aren't making money unless a major network shows a fight. The fight promoter has to pay for the venue, insurance, security, medical services, sanctioning fees, and the opponent's purse, so the only way for the fighter to get paid is if a network puts up enough money to cover all of this and *then* have some left over for them.

None of these costs are optional, but the opponent's purse is a slightly more complicated issue. Every fight has an "A-side" (the expected winner) and a "B-side" (the expected loser). On small shows used for local entertainment or to develop fighters, the A-side is either the hometown favorite and expected driver of ticket sales, the guy with a promoter or financial backer, or both. Some A-side fighters only fit into one of those categories, but many guys have both. Regardless of which slot the A-side falls into, he's responsible for covering the cost of the B-side.

The B-side needs to get paid for fighting. He will also need his travel expenses, food, and hotel room covered. The B-side fighter's cost depends on his record and how dangerous the A-side is. The better the record the B-side has, the more money he wants. From his perspective, you'd only be calling him if you expect him to lose, so he's gotta make sure that the loss is worth it, because every defeat diminishes his earning capacity.

The A-side's record doesn't matter nearly as much as how he got that record. A 12–0 fighter with twelve knockouts will have to pay more than a 12–0 fighter who won all his fights by decision. If a boxer doesn't want to—or can't, due to lackluster ticket sales—cover his opponent's purse, he'll be matched as someone's B-side and try to pull an upset.

The economics of club-level professional boxing are challenging. Fighters often struggle to sell enough tickets to cover their opponent's costs. Many small-time promoters are promoters in name only, leaving the boxer to do all the legwork. As a novice pro, I experienced this firsthand. For my January 2013 debut in Steubenville, Ohio, an hour from my home in Pittsburgh, I wore multiple hats:

1. Fighter: training rigorously while working thirty hours a week.

2. Promoter and marketer: spending days messaging and promoting the fight on social media.

3. Ticket seller: driving around at night after practice to deliver thirty-five-dollar tickets. (This was before Cash App existed and Venmo went mainstream, making ticket sales even more time-consuming.)

The challenge for me was convincing people to drive an hour for an event that, if successful, wouldn't last long. After weeks of me juggling these roles, January 26, 2013, arrived. Regardless of the outcome, I could finally call myself a professional athlete.

Win the Fight Before You Go to War

I was the last fight of the night. Normally, that's the most coveted spot on a professional boxing card; it's the main event. But fighting at a Serbian American cultural center in the middle of Ohio took the shine away. Instead, it just meant I'd have to wait longer to get this over with.

As I warmed up, I was focused, with a low but noticeable level of anxiety. I felt like I was taking a difficult test that I had studied for but that only had a pass rate of 50 percent. Someone had to lose this fight; despite my experience and preparation, it could be me. My amateur accomplishments would mean nothing if Jon Hill wiped the floor with me.

When you get in the ring, you're not afraid of losing, getting hurt, or even dying. You're afraid of the other man dancing over your corpse while the body is still fresh. If his celebration of your failure is a deep stab wound to your pride, then the knife twist is the audience's reaction. In the mind of the fighter, a loss reduces him to nothing.

Boxing had become my identity. It had become the special something that made people pay attention to me—but it was more than just the attention that I liked. Boxing brought me respect and admiration. It had taken me all around the country and saved me from homelessness. If I lost my pro debut, though, I would just be a broke dude in his twenties with an alcohol problem.

As I walked to the ring, I tried to block out the sounds of people cheering for me. I didn't make eye contact with anyone because I didn't want to lose my concentration, even though it was impossible to think of anything else. I saved my eye contact for the staredown with Jon Hill.

In the ancient classic on warfare strategy *The Art of War*, Sun Tzu said, "Victorious warriors win first and then go to war, while defeated warriors go to war first and then seek to win." This psychological warfare is the purpose of the staredown between two fighters before every boxing match, as the referee goes over the rules and the fighters touch gloves before the fight begins. It is a mental attempt to elicit fear in the opponent and simultaneously disguise any sign of your own fear. It's your attempt to win the fight before you go to war.

> I keep my eyes on him. Then once I see a chink in his armor, "boom," then I know I have him. When he comes to the center of the ring, he still looks at me with this piercing look as if he's not afraid, but he already made that mistake when he looked down for that one-tenth of a second. I know I have him. He'll fight hard for the first two or three rounds, but I already know I broke his spirit.

This is how former heavyweight champion and "baddest man on the planet" Mike Tyson described the power of the fear generated during the staredown. Mike Tyson was a punishing boxer, but his reputation and approach in the ring won many fights before they started. I don't know if I intimated Jon Hill, but he didn't intimidate me. I remembered that I had the experience and the pedigree, and I remembered the sacrifices I'd made and risks I had taken to get to this point.

A Partnership Only Works If You Trust Your Partner

In the first round, we felt each other out. Neither of us landed any significant blows, but he tagged me a few times with his jab and was moving out of the way before I could answer back. While it was an uneventful round, it was important because it was my first taste of professional boxing.

"Good job," Tom said in our corner. "Your first pro round is in the books. You ain't a rookie anymore. Now start pumpin' your jab in his face and putting pressure on him. This guy can't fight moving backward. Get in his chest like you did Dominic."

Tom was reminding me to fight him like I fought Dominic Breazeale at the Golden Gloves tournament. The same style had gotten me this far, but confronted with the newness of a professional fight, I was fighting cautiously. I went out in the second round with an aim to fight true to my style and temperament. While I was closing the distance to land a hook to his liver, though, Hill hit me with a perfectly timed left cross that made my knees buckle as I fell into him.

This was the first time I'd ever been dazed in a fight. I'd been hurt in fights before, but pain is easy to deal with. You just ignore it and keep pushing through it. When your nervous system gets scrambled from a shot and you feel your legs wobble, that's a different story. There isn't much you can do except hold on and wait for your brain to sort things out.

That's exactly what I did. I clinched until the ref separated us, which was just enough time for me to regain my bearings. I don't think Jon was aware that he had stunned me, because he didn't jump right on after the ref separated us, buying me a few precious seconds to recuperate. Just as I began to reengage, the bell rang to signal the end of the second round.

"You got rocked and probably lost that round," Tom told me as

I applied a cold stainless-steel block known as an "end swell" beneath my eyes. The block does exactly that—it ends the swelling that fighters experience in the middle of the fight, to ensure that the injury doesn't interfere with vision or get big enough to be easily cut.

"Look here. Every time he jabs, he drops his left hand. So, the next time he jabs, just throw a right hand from hell."

In the heat of battle, the coach is like a general who sees the entire battlefield and develops a strategy. The fighter is like a soldier in the trenches who follows this plan. The battle is easier to win if the soldier trusts the general's plan and the general trusts his soldiers to execute. The last time Tom had told me how to exploit a weakness he spotted, I scored a knockout. I trusted this time would be no different.

The third round began, and Hill was tentative. Although he had gotten me good in the last round, he had also tasted my power on a few exchanges and wasn't eager for a second helping. Then he jabbed. I slipped to the outside of it and launched a right cross around his glove that sent him wobbling around the ring until he fell over. I held my breath, hoping he wouldn't rise before the referee reached ten. He got up just before nine.

When it was clear that the referee would let the fight continue, I heard Tom shout, "Now do it again, dammit!"

I let my right hand go without hesitation. Hill hit the canvas face down this time, and the referee frantically waved his arms, signaling the end of the fight. I must have still been holding my breath, because I let out a huge sigh of relief.

I had won my professional debut in a spectacular way—by a

third-round KO. I shared the news on Facebook before I even got changed, and then I geared up for my favorite way to celebrate: drinking to the point where I'd regret any text messages that I sent, then sleeping off the hangover the next day.

Acting Like a Tough Guy Invites People to See How Tough You Really Are

I fought two more times before leaving for basic training in June, winning both fights by knockout. I posted videos of each fight on Facebook to promote the next one. Posting these videos also made me a small-time local celebrity, the best part of which was that it allowed me to drink for free at several bars near where I lived.

Now, I had no delusions of grandeur about all of this. I wasn't a world-class boxer. Unless you knew me from the bar or Facebook, no one knew who I was. Even if they met me while I was out drinking, they didn't know I fought unless someone told them. I did a lot of things when I drank, but I didn't brag about boxing. Part of this was just my personality—I liked being seen as an interesting conversationalist, unless it just happened to come out that I beat people up for money. But the real reason was a matter of safety.

For some weird reason, whenever a guy gets drunk and decides to pick a fight, he never goes after a guy his size or smaller. Every time, without fail, he picks a bigger guy. I had avoided

enough bar fights in my time to know that showing off your tough-
ness was the surest way to attract the violent attention of someone
who wanted to test it out. While I couldn't do anything about my
size, I could downplay anything about myself that made me seem
like a tough guy. That meant not mentioning my fighting.

This didn't always work, especially when people introduced
me as "that guy who fights people for a living." That type of in-
troduction always led to at least one guy who wanted to see if
he could take a punch from me, so he could tell all his friends he
got punched by a professional boxer. I always declined. People have
no idea what it's like to get hit by someone trained to throw a
punch—especially someone who weighs 225 pounds.

One time, I was partying with a guy we'll call "Ace." Ace had
been competing in MMA for years. Some guy at the party got in
his face over something, and Ace hit the guy in the face with a
crisp one-two. The guy fell backward instantly, with his head hitting the pavement first. Ace was lucky that the guy only ended up
with a concussion, because you can easily die that way.

If the guy had died, Ace would have had to prove that the
punch was in self-defense. If he couldn't do that, the best-case
scenario for him would have been an involuntary manslaughter
charge and a three-to-five-year prison sentence. While I believe it's
better to be "judged by twelve than carried by six," I went out of
my way to avoid any situation that would force me to choose between potentially killing someone or being killed.

Coping with Your Problems
Only Makes Them Worse

Despite my taste of success in the ring, though, things weren't going so well outside of it. I spent so much time drinking that it became difficult to function when I wasn't drinking. I drank before I went to work, and there was a bar across the street from my T-Mobile store, so I'd go drink on my break. During my shift, I texted my friends to see who was up for getting drunk after I finished working. If no one was available to party, I'd go drink by myself at one of the bars where getting free drinks was the norm.

Eventually, I started leaving boxing practice early to make it to happy hours. Then it became missing practice, telling my coach I wasn't feeling well or had a car problem. Of course, the only problem I had was an alcohol problem. I realized that I was putting my boxing career at risk, so rather than stop drinking and focus on my training, I started drinking before practice.

"Hey, come here," Tom said after I had just finished a round in my last sparring session before heading to basic training. The tone of his voice told me something was wrong. He took a quick sniff.

"Are you fuckin' drinkin' at the gym?"

"What? No, I just had a few beers before I came here. I'm cool." Tom lost it.

"I've seen a lot of dumb shit, but I ain't ever seen a guy drinking before sparring. Are you fuckin' stupid?" I was twenty-eight, and he was scolding me like a teenager who had just gotten into his father's liquor cabinet. I just stood there in the corner of the ring, taking it.

"Yo, Adam! We're done." He was shouting to Adam Milstead, a former star in the UFC light heavyweight division who was one of my sparring partners. "This asshole has been drinking. He doesn't care about getting better."

I left the gym that day and sat at the bar by myself for the evening. I didn't call any friends to see if they wanted to join me. I just nursed a few drinks and thought about my life. Outside of boxing, I hadn't done anything with it, and now my drinking problem was so bad that I was putting even boxing in danger. I imagined how things would be in five years. Would I have more options or fewer? Would I be a champion, or would I be in the Fighter's Graveyard? Would I get this alcohol problem under control, or would it cost me my freedom—or my life?

I craved acceptance. I had always wanted to fit in and be considered a "cool kid." When I harnessed this drive into something constructive, I pushed myself to the edges of my physical, mental, and emotional development. It's one of the things that drove me to take up boxing: If the virtues of my innate personality weren't enough for me to fit in, I would try to earn approval with my achievements.

When my need for acceptance led me down the path of least resistance, I found myself spiraling into alcoholism and self-destructive behavior. I tried to be the guy who drank more than everyone else, the life of the party. Every time someone cheered me on or invited me to another night of heavy drinking, it fed my craving for recognition. But now, I was drinking way beyond seeking acceptance—it was teetering on the edge of costing me everything I'd worked so hard to achieve.

In my final days before heading to basic training, I had a few beers but didn't get drunk. Instead of drowning myself in alcohol, I avoided the bars and took it easy. I knew I'd already put my boxing career at risk; I wasn't about to jeopardize my enlistment and future plans too. God willing, five years would pass, and I wanted to give myself the best shot at a future that didn't end in the Fighter's Graveyard—or worse. Getting through basic training was the first step toward that future.

X

Make Your Reality Match Your Ego

Afeter our flights landed in the St. Louis airport, all the recruits waited in the airport's United Services Organization (USO) lounge to be picked up by a charter bus for the two-and-a-half-hour drive to Fort Leonard Wood. I wanted to make the most of my time, so I wrote this post on one of the open computers:

> This post is short. I don't have much time. I'm in St. Louis, and a bus leaves in an hour to take me off the grid for 10–12 weeks. I had so many ideas floating around in my head to write my final post on, but so many options stressed me out. Originally, there wasn't going to be a final post because there were many other pressing matters, and my writing was not one of them.

But who am I to deprive the good people of the lessons I learn from my unusual life?

I remember a conversation I had with a drinking buddy about my plan to return to school. The basics of the plan had me starting around 29 and not finishing until 32—that is an optimistic estimate considering the other demands I'll have. I suggested he do something similar. His response—a man of my age, 28—was that he didn't want to waste the time because he'd be too old.

This saddened me because no matter what happens, he will turn 32. Either he turns 32 with a degree and more options, or he doesn't, but in his mind, it's already too late.

Compare this to one of the most inspiring moments I've ever had with another person. A few years ago, I ran into a guy I studied jiujitsu with. He was out on the town with his cute girlfriend—she was 21—celebrating his recent graduation from college. He was 32. He started at 28 and got a bachelor's in Mathematics and Computer Science. These are not easy degrees to obtain.

The lesson here is obvious: beautiful young women love ambition. The other obvious lesson—more relevant to this post—is that it's only too late to go after what you want when you are no longer breathing.

I didn't start boxing until I was 22, which is pretty late considering I had zero combat sports experience. Yet, I have won a national title, beat an Olympian, and made more money as an amateur than most professionals make in their entire careers. This would have never happened if I had decided 22 was too old to start boxing.

Time is the most valuable commodity there is. I've stated this before. No matter how late you get on track, it's never too late to use it wisely and to your advantage. Sure, it will be more difficult, but anything worth doing is usually difficult. The road to mediocrity is paved with unchallenging tasks.

My current challenges are sitting behind me, literally. As I write this, I'm waiting for the bus to take me to basic training with a bunch of kids who are, on average, age 19 and range from 17 to 20. I suspect this will be the norm of my life for the next six years since I'll be enrolling in college when I return. It's a little intimidating until I remember that most people will never put themselves in such an uncomfortable position.

There are many things that people want to attempt, but they believe that their time has passed. There are lots of reasons for this. Things like school and sports are largely considered a young person's game, and to a degree, they are. But that degree is much smaller than we're led to believe.

I'd say the only limitation a person really has is that the body eventually deteriorates to a point where competition against the top levels is impossible. But once again, this is a lot later than people want you to think.

The future is coming regardless of what you do. You can either do something to prepare and reap the benefits or complain about how it's always too late. One guy goes back to school at 28, and the other says 28 is too old. One is rewarded with a cute young woman, and one is doing nothing as a wage slave.

My friends, I leave with one of the most real talk rap lyrics I've ever heard. T. I. said it best,

"So I guess the moral of this here class is
Life's who makes it, not about who makes it the fastest."

Looking back over that post, two things stand out to me. The first is that I'm a much better writer now. It's incredible how much better you can get at something if you consistently practice. The second thing that jumps out at me is the combination of confidence, nervousness, and dedication I expressed.

The book *The Triple Package: How Three Unlikely Traits Explain the Rise and Fall of Cultural Groups in America* explores how a particular combination of traits leads to tremendous success. The book says that the success of minority groups in America is rooted in the combination of a superiority complex, inferiority complex, and conscientiousness. (The book uses different words, but the idea is the same.) You must simultaneously believe that you're better than everyone around you and deserve more while also working like you have something to prove. Or, as I like to say it, you have to think you're the shit while thinking that you ain't shit at all—then bust your ass to prove the first part right and the second part wrong.

That's how I've always thought of it, but then I heard the idea expressed even better. My friend, the author, businessman, and podcaster Hotep Jesus (real name Bryan Sharpe), discusses his time working as a server at different chain restaurants. While working in that industry, he never accepted his situation, but it deeply bothered him that he wasn't progressing toward his goals. Speaking about his thought process at the time, he says: "My ego is inflated, but I'm looking at my life, and I'm like, 'How come my life doesn't reflect my ego?' I know I'm great, but my bank account doesn't reflect that. My life doesn't reflect it either."

Identical feelings had led me to this point. I wanted to be more than a small-time club show boxer with an alcohol problem, working a minimum-wage job. The next step on my journey was how I believed I'd make this happen.

Everything takes longer than you plan, never happens the way you want, and always gets worse before it gets better. This is not a bug. It's a feature, to weed out people who are just paying lip service to the idea of self-improvement and who don't want to do the work.

Your Life Will Be Shit as Long as You Keep Bullshitting Yourself

"Shut the fuck up and get the fuck off the bus."

Those were the first words I heard when a drill sergeant stepped onto the bus at Fort Leonard Wood. During the entire ride, most of the recruits joked and laughed with one another. Now, everyone was silent as shit got real.

It was 12:30 a.m., but the drill sergeants wasted no time issuing uniforms and packing away our cell phones, laptops, and any other contraband we had brought. We stored everything in a bag with our names on it.

"What the fuck is this?" a woman yelled at me as she emptied my book bag.

"My recruiter told me I'd have time to skip rope and—"

"Not here. Pack that shit away!"

The first night of processing was like the American TSA: There was lots of yelling, and no matter how fast you moved, it was never fast enough—and there was nothing you could do about it. Processing took almost two hours before we got to sleep, but we still had to wake up at 5:00 a.m. for morning physical training (PT).

Basic training is nine weeks long, plus one week of "reception" at the beginning. Calling your first week in the army "reception" is technically correct but colloquially misleading. In reception, you're not even a recruit, but the military is responsible for you. You have to get processed, pick up all the gear you'll be issued, go through a conveyor belt of immunizations, and get your hair shaved off. Your only access to the world is one phone call from a pay phone you're allowed to make halfway through the week. If you don't have any phone numbers memorized, you're shit out of luck. If you write any letters home, you won't receive a response for weeks, because you haven't even been assigned to the platoon and company where you'll go through basic training. This means you don't even have an address for any incoming mail.

I can understand why an eighteen-year-old who'd never been away from home might have trouble adjusting, but for me, the worst part of reception was the extremes. Some parts of reception were rigidly structured, like the two minutes we had for meal-time, the strict 5:00 a.m. wake-ups, and the PT. But when we weren't scheduled to do anything, there was mind-numbing boredom. The Bible is the only book you can read in basic training, and you only get that when basic training officially starts.

The following nine weeks were basic training. While I was rarely bored during marches, I spent a lot of time thinking and reflecting on everything in my life that had led me there. My reason for enlisting was simple enough: I saw college as the way out of dead-end jobs, and joining the military was the only way I could afford to pay for college. I chose the National Guard, as it allowed me to go to school and box. But how did I get to the point where, at twenty-eight, I felt like this was my best option?

Every problem that I'd ever had in my life kept coming back to alcohol. If you took away boxing, I never dedicated myself to anything long enough to reap any benefits. I was terrible with money and was so broke that when I moved back to Pittsburgh from LA, the only reason I wasn't homeless was because Matt and Bill let me rent a room for two hundred dollars a month, something I never would've found elsewhere.

So I couldn't afford a normal rent—but I could always find money for alcohol. I always thought I didn't have time to better myself—but I always had time for happy hours. I wanted to be a better fighter—but for the past year, I had arranged my boxing schedule around being able to drink with my friends.

Going further back, I thought about how I was raised. Children who grow up in abusive homes and adverse environments are far more likely to end up with addiction issues. If your childhood is full of traumatic episodes, trauma responses (including addiction) remain your default mode of acting and thinking into adulthood—and there's a good chance you'll repeat the cycle when you're an adult. I fit that pattern perfectly.

I handwrote these reflections and mailed them home to a friend, who uploaded them to my website, where they were automatically reposted to Twitter and Facebook. A few years before, I had started a website where I wrote essays about my life, just to get things off my chest despite not having many people to talk to. By now, I had a small but loyal audience of a few hundred followers who were learning from my writing as I was learning about my life. (These old essays are no longer on my website, but I was able to access them via the Wayback Machine.) Writing down my life story has helped me learn more about myself.

I'm the first person to say that once you're an adult, your childhood is no longer an excuse. With that said, I understand the power of the environment you're raised in. My life was my responsibility, but that didn't negate the influence of my early environment. I couldn't do anything about the past, but by accepting the truth of my present circumstances, I could improve the future.

Although I had joined the army to improve my employment prospects, the unintended benefit was that I cut myself off from the environment that enabled my heavy drinking. This was an environment that I had fostered with every decision I made, but now I had time away, to start a recovery process that I hadn't planned for but desperately needed. Boxing had taught me that I could be the master of my own destiny, and I had finally decided to apply that lesson beyond the ring.

Your Weaknesses Don't Have to Be Your Destiny

Most of the army's basic combat training (BCT) is simple. You just have to follow the rules and pass the physical fitness test. The rules are simple and clearly explained: Be where you're supposed to be when you're supposed to be there, dressed and groomed to the military standard, and don't ever get caught sleeping any time or place you aren't authorized to do so.

The physical fitness tests have changed since I was in, but in 2013, your performance was based on a timed two-mile run and the number of push-ups and sit-ups you could do in two minutes.

If you weren't in shape enough to pass the tests when you arrived, the daily 5:00 a.m. PT would guarantee that by the end of your ten weeks there, you'd at least be able to get a passing score. The requirements were based on your age, and while your average couch potato would likely fail, you didn't need to be a professional athlete to get through. If you were one, like I was, it was a breeze.

For my age bracket, the maximum passing time for the two-mile run was 15:54. In my training, it was a bad day if I did anything slower than thirteen minutes. But most of the recruits weren't close to my time, despite being ten years younger. I also blasted through my push-ups, regularly knocking out sixty—ten over the required minimum for my age. Sit-ups were more challenging, because I carried so much of my 225 pounds in my upper body, but I still passed the test.

The part of BCT that gave many of the recruits a challenge was being away from home for so long. Most of them had just turned eighteen and had never gone so long without seeing their friends and family, or, if they didn't see them, at least being able to quickly call or text. When we had our precious few moments of free time, we could write as many letters as we wanted, but throughout BCT we were only allowed to make three phone calls, spaced at three-week intervals, with the final one marking the return of your cell phone and connection to the world.

It would have been difficult for me if I had enlisted before living in Los Angeles. However, my move there was abrupt, and for the fifteen months I was there, I mostly lived alone, hardly socialized with the other fighters, and saw my friends from home twice: once when I flew back over the holidays and again when they flew out to visit. For me, BCT wasn't even lonely. I was just with unfamiliar people who were mostly a decade younger than me.

There was one part of basic training where their youth was an asset, and my experience from boxing was a liability: shooting. Although twenty-eight is young to start having age-related nearsightedness, the thousands of punches I had taken over the past five years accelerated the decline of my eyes. This damage was a problem when we started learning how to shoot.

Basic rifle marksmanship (BRM) was the one part of BCT that gave me trouble. It didn't matter how well you followed orders, how fast you ran, or how many push-ups you could do—if you couldn't shoot, you were a useless soldier, and the army didn't want you. A large portion of enlisted army recruits are from rural areas where shooting guns is a part of life. For those kids, the marksmanship part of basic training was as easy as the running was for me.

No matter how much previous shooting experience a civilian has before joining the army, they've still likely never fired the army's standard-issue M16, so we received nearly five weeks of training with the weapon, learning everything about it: how to clean, disassemble, and reassemble it; how to load magazines and deal with a jammed round. All these rote skills are easy to learn and execute and come in handy when it's time to shoot, but they still don't pass you through basic training. Only passing the marksmanship test does, and that's where my problems began.

To pass the test, you have to hit twenty-three of forty targets that pop up at distances of one hundred, two hundred, and three hundred yards away. You can use any seated firing position and get no extra points for hitting farther targets; while it's impossible to pass the test without hitting some of the three-hundred-yard targets, you won't fail if you don't hit them all.

We first had practice sessions on virtual gun ranges before heading to the live gun ranges. You didn't have to shoot on the qualification days if you hit twenty-three targets during the live-ammunition practice session. Twenty-three out of forty is only 57.5 percent, which maybe seems low as a success rate, but think about it this way: At that rate, if you fire two shots, one will hit. Even if that shot isn't lethal, a bullet from an M16 will neutralize the target's ability to fight back. One in two doesn't seem too bad when that one can remove a limb or put someone in a wheelchair.

If you have ever taken any exam, passing a test where the minimum required score is 57 percent is generally no problem. On the surface, the BRM test is no different: You aim at targets, hit a few more than half, and go home happy. But if you dig deeper, BRM has its fair share of problems.

For starters, there is the penalty for failure. Hit fewer than twenty-three targets, and the military slaps you with an NSO—a "New Start Over." This designation is exactly what it sounds like: You will start your basic training *all over.* The BRM test isn't given until the sixth week of training, so there's the possibility that you'll have to restart all the way from the beginning, setting you back nearly two months.

Granted, starting over from the beginning is only one possible outcome. If the timing lines up, sometimes recruits are merely put into another company that's just about to start their BRM training phase, about four weeks into BCT. Either way, failing means that you will be at BCT for at least three more weeks and, in many cases, much longer. BCT is already ten weeks long—no one wants to stay any longer than necessary. On top of that, it's depressing as hell to tell everyone you flunked and got held back.

I had entered the army with a plan to attend school, and everything was timed perfectly: I'd finish my training by the end of December, I figured, allowing me to start school in January. However, if I failed BRM, my enrollment would be delayed until at least September. Failing here meant a setback of nearly a year in starting school.

The week before the test, things were looking bad. On all six live-fire practice rounds, my best score was twenty-one—and that was an outlier. My other scores ranged from nine to eighteen. On qualification day, I had to *really* try.

Blocking out my fears of failure was already difficult, but shooting on a cloudless, 94-degree day only worsened it. My first attempt—out of three—was a dismal failure, hitting only fifteen targets. I struggled to focus: When I missed a target, I couldn't let go of the failure. Instead of clearing my mind and focusing on the next shot, I tried to correct each mistake as I went. This approach broke from the fundamentals we'd been taught—I wasn't patient; I wasn't shooting with care. Every missed shot felt like a ghost, haunting the next. My score plummeted, and with it, my confidence. My heart sank into my stomach, and I failed the second attempt too. Now, with just one chance left, I felt my future was hanging by a thread.

I limped back to the air-conditioned cooldown area, where my comrades, who had already passed, were waiting for me.

"I'm going to fail," I said. "It's too hot to focus, and the sun keeps burning my eyes. Shit!"

"Stop thinking all that shit, man," responded Private Long, one of my bunkmates. "You said you were a pro fighter, right? Don't you guys know how to focus through painful shit?"

Long was one of those kids who had experience shooting, although he was from Miami. His advantage came from a military father who had taught him how to shoot.

"Yeah, just focus on taking the next shot," followed up Private Louviere, in his Southern drawl. "Fuck everything else." There were a lot of boys from the bayou country in Louisiana with French last names who had spent a lot of time shooting. Louviere had qualified on the first practice run, hitting thirty-four targets.

They were right, I realized. This should be no different than how I approached boxing. In a fight, I could zone in and block out external thoughts and fears, crowd noise, and pain. I had the power to shoot well, even if my eyes were bothering me. I just needed to breathe, focus, and live in the moment. No more thoughts about getting out, drinking beer, seeing friends, and starting school. I would just focus on each target as it popped up, shoot, and move to the next with no thought of the previous shot. In other words, I would live in the present moment and shoot from there.

It was 94 degrees with 85 percent humidity, and I was staring a significant setback in the face. I was using precious mental energy to ignore the swampy air by thinking of the air-conditioned waiting room, but I needed to focus on what was in front of me. My elbows ached from being in the unsupported prone firing position, and my neck stung as sweat dripped into bug bites that had accumulated throughout the day. My eyes burned with sweat, but I focused through the discomfort and got ready for my final attempt.

The targets came and went. I didn't bother counting how many dropped from my shots. My palms had tiny, painful burns. My focus was so intense that I didn't notice that at one point I had touched the hot gun barrel. I walked to the scorekeeper, fully prepared to need something to treat the emotional burns I would have as well.

"Private Latimore. Twenty-six out of forty. Pass."

My stomach and heart found their way back to their rightful place. Assuming nothing unexpected or crazy happened, I'd graduate . . . on time!

Everything was still moving according to plan.

BRM is the only part of BCT where failure isn't an option. Once I conquered that, everything else fell into place for graduation. But there was still one more test ahead—one the army couldn't prepare me for. All they did was strip away my ability to run from it, leaving me with no choice but to face it head-on.

There's Nothing Wrong with Being Afraid

I've always been afraid of getting struck by lightning. I've never called it an irrational fear or phobia, because an average of 270 people are struck by lightning every year. Sure, the odds are low that I would be one of them, but everyone has been in a thunderstorm. I think it's weird that more people aren't afraid of getting hit by a random bolt of electricity from the sky.

My earliest memory of confronting this fear was at a sleep-away camp when I was seven. I went on a weeklong camping trip with the Hill District YMCA. When we got to our site, the girls set up in a flat grass clearing right on the edge of where the thick forest brush started. The boys set up about 100 yards away, right on the edge of a beautiful creek. The sound of rushing water seemed like it would be a lovely sound to fall asleep to.

On the first night, though, a thunderstorm dropped so much rain so quickly that the creek flooded into our campsite. In the dead of night, with nothing but frequent lightning illuminating the way, the boys had to scramble down to the girls' camp to seek shelter.

On the way, I twisted my ankle so badly I thought I had broken it. I spent the rest of the trip sleeping on the ground in the same clothes because my stuff was soaked, and the humidity made it impossible to dry out. I also refused to poop for seven days, because the outhouse had no lights, was full of insects, and nearly overflowed with backed-up human waste. Ever since this highly unpleasant event, I feared being outside during lightning.

By themselves, thunderstorms didn't scare me. I've always loved falling asleep to rumbling thunder and the sound of heavy raindrops on the roof. As long as I was in the house, I wasn't afraid of lightning either. Only when I was outside did lightning make me so scared that I would run until I passed out to take shelter. This happened once at a summer barbecue at a state park when I was twenty. Another time, when I got caught in a storm coming home from a free karate class, I waited on a stranger's porch until it passed. (When I did this, a kind old lady came out and gave me cookies and water but told me that she wanted me off of her porch by nightfall or she was calling the cops.)

Fort Leonard Wood is located in a part of the United States called "Tornado Alley." The area is named as such because 75 percent of the world's tornadoes touch down in the region. To get tornadoes, you need strong thunderstorms, which always have a *lot* of lightning. When the sky darkened over the fort, I could no longer run until my body dropped or take cover until it passed. I couldn't do much of anything unless an officer or noncommissioned officer (NCO) ordered me to. The summer weather in Missouri was either stiflingly hot or terrifyingly violent, but training almost always goes on. After all, you can't control the weather on the battlefield, so you have to learn to control how you react to it.

This was another lesson I had learned in the ring that I was reminded of in the military. Every fighter is scared—any fighter who says otherwise is either lying or a psychopath. One way we deal with that fear is through a lot of sparring. Sparring makes you comfortable with the chaos of a fight in a safe environment. The more you put yourself through the dangers of sparring, the more comfortable you are in a real fight. And the more comfortable you are, the less likely you are to freeze or flee out of fear.

The forced daily confrontation with severe weather slowly built up my psychological resilience. Whenever I marched under a storm and nothing happened, I became more confident that nothing would ever happen. While this isn't exactly true—people do still get struck by lightning—it made me less afraid and more relaxed when the sky darkened. Whatever you're scared of is almost always worse in your imagination because, in your mind, the worst-case scenario always goes down in the worst way possible. But in real life, this isn't how things tend to happen.

In my mind, it was a guarantee that I'd be struck by lightning if I weren't in a building. I imagined that one day, I'd be walking outside during a storm, and suddenly I'd wake up in the hospital covered with burns, after being in a weeklong coma. The reality is that my odds of being struck by lightning are 1 in 15,000. To put that number into perspective, I'd have to walk outside during a thunderstorm every day for forty-one years to get struck once.

By the eighth week of BCT, I was comfortable outside during the stormiest weather. It's a good thing that I was, because week eight was a weeklong field training exercise: We'd live and train away from our barracks to learn how to set up and run a forward operating base. During a vicious storm, we conducted the twenty-five-mile march to the training site in full battle gear. The storm had the type of lightning that would have previously terrified me. However, this time I felt calm and in control during it all. And, as if the army had engineered horrible conditions just to test us, the skies cleared up as soon as we arrived. But it turned out the biggest test of my newfound courage was yet to come.

In BCT, you have to do "fire guard": Every night, at least two recruits from the platoon must be awake at any given time. Duties include patrolling the barracks area, keeping an eye out for fires, and watching for fellow recruits attempting to leave the barracks area. Of course, there were never any threats, as we were on a training base, but the exercise was preparation in case you were deployed to a place where these things could happen.

On our first night in the field, I drew the straw for the third shift, which meant I'd get about two hours of sleep before I started. However, I woke up earlier than expected because my sleeping bag felt wet. At first, I thought I was just dreaming, but the recruit I was set to replace on the next fire guard was tapping me on the shoulder.

"Damn, did I oversleep?"

"Nah. Fire guard is canceled. The weather is too shitty outside."

I looked up and saw him standing there, drenched. It wasn't a dream—I realized our sleeping area at the bottom of the slope was slowly filling with water. A crack of thunder jolted me fully awake. The violent weather from our earlier march had returned with a vengeance while I slept. The rain was pounding harder, the wind was fierce, and the thunder was deafening.

We stayed in our shelter, wide awake, waiting for the storm to pass, but the calm never came. And even if it did, everything around us was submerged. We were standing on our gear, waiting for an order to evacuate that never came. As the water continued to rise, we had no choice but to abandon our shelter and head for the covered tables where meals were served. Other platoons were already gathered there, as the entire hillside of shelters was in various stages of flooding.

Stepping out into the storm, I was immediately overwhelmed by the lightning overhead. The sky was so lit up that I could read the name tags on my fellow recruits' uniforms. Each flash made everything unnervingly clear, like a strobe light at some twisted party. My old fears surged back, and I lost my composure. I started running, only to stumble and cut my hand on a cluster of rocks. The fall felt surreal, as if it happened in slow motion, disorienting me even more with each burst of light.

Lying there, I realized I had to pull myself together. If I didn't calm down, I knew I'd end up seriously hurt—maybe tripping over something, falling again, even smashing a tooth. I forced myself to breathe and accept that I could die. That acceptance brought an unexpected calm: The worst that could happen was that it would all end. Confronting that fear, I reclaimed control.

I looked up at the sky again, this time with a sense of awe and appreciation. I marveled at how peaceful I felt, even enjoying the lightning show, privileged to witness nature's raw power up close. But that peace was fleeting.

"Tornado! Tornado! Get in the shelters!"

We spent the night in the bunkers. I woke up with a stiff neck and a sore ass from sleeping hunched in a concrete corner and trying not to lie on anyone else. We were packed in there, but I still found a little space to drift off in peace for three hours before morning came.

Later, I checked the weather for that night. While there was no confirmed tornado touchdown, six inches of rain had fallen in six hours. The field exercise site was so severely damaged by the rain that we returned to the barracks to sleep for the next two nights.

I don't think I would have been able to survive that night if I hadn't been forced to confront my fear during the marches. The storms became part of the environment. I didn't plan for them to be there, but I controlled myself, stayed focused, and kept myself from getting hurt.

Everyone had different challenges in basic training. Mine were shooting and lightning. I conquered them both, which gave me confidence and faith in myself that, in many ways, exceeded what I had experienced when I started boxing.

I graduated from basic training two weeks after surviving that storm. I was no longer a recruit but a soldier, and I started the next leg of my journey to make my reality match my ego. For the next twenty-two weeks, I'd be at Fort Gregg-Adams. Ironically, in an environment without any alcohol, I'd learn the most about what had driven me to alcoholism.

Never Be So Sure of What You Want That You Wouldn't Take Something Better

During the ten weeks of basic training, every recruit learns the fundamentals of being a soldier. We're taught how to shoot, administer first aid, set up and secure a forward operating base, and follow orders. In the modern era of combat, though, various skills and abilities are required to support the army's mission. To meet these demands, every soldier selects a military occupational specialty most suited to their strengths, temperaments, and capabilities.

After completing basic training, I attended advanced individual training for twenty-two weeks to become a land combat electronic missile system repairer. Because that lengthy title is a mouthful, we usually refer to the job by its military occupational code—"ninety-four alpha" or "94A."

The 94A performs support-level maintenance on some of the army's most powerful weapons systems. The work required a secret clearance, which meant a thorough background check and a three-hour interview explaining gaps in my employment, overdue bills, or low-level criminal offenses.

One day during BCT, an officer pulled me out of training for the interview. I had to explain what I was doing in California, how I let my credit score get so low, and the nature of my year-long driver's-license suspension. I was fortunate that I hadn't been arrested for breaking any laws. Many convictions bar you from enlistment entirely; for the permissible convictions, you're banned from any military jobs requiring secret or top-secret clearance. I'd been reckless but lucky. I thought of this as a second chance, as well as a sign.

Think of 94As as electricians for the military. To work on the electrical systems of the nation's weapons systems, we had to become familiar with the basics of electronics. As with marksmanship training, the military assumed no prior knowledge of electronics besides the information tested on the ASVAB.

For the first six weeks of AIT, I underwent basic electronic maintenance training (BMET). I learned the rudimentary techniques of circuit building, troubleshooting, and electronic theory. All the assignments were hands-on, but I was also tested on my ability to use math to solve electrical problems. Everything I learned was practical knowledge that would be useful outside of the military. This is where I changed my mind about my course of study in school.

My original plan had been to get a degree in applied mathematics. I initially wanted an engineering degree, because it seemed to offer a more direct path to a higher-paying job. However, attaining those degrees meant I'd have to go through a heavy dose of lab-based science classes. I wasn't worried about my intellectual ability to do the work—instead, I figured that with fighting and having a job, I wouldn't be able to make all the labs.

I was already anticipating missing classes because of my training schedule, but that was fine, because I thought I'd just explain my situation to my professors, show up for exams, and do a lot of self-study. Lab classes wouldn't allow that, so I put the idea out of my head. But now that I saw how fun and useful this course of study was, my mindset changed.

To prepare for this challenge, I took advantage of my freedom at AIT and ordered two books on Amazon: *Schaum's 3000 Solved Problems in Calculus* and *Schaum's 3000 Solved Problems in Physics*. I spent most of my free time at AIT working on the problems in these books to continue shoring up my math skills.

I wasn't worried about chemistry, because I knew from high school that I could make it through that course with memorization. There was a lab component, but now I was confident that I would be betting on myself and crossing that bridge when the time came.

Attention Looks Like Respect to People Not Used to Receiving Either

In basic training, it's difficult to build genuine friendships. While you spend every moment with your fellow recruits, overcoming challenges and difficulties that allow you to bond with people quickly, you can't get to know someone in depth. Talking and socializing are only allowed for one hour before bed. Yes, there are places to steal conversation, but you never get to connect with people. AIT is different.

In AIT, you still aren't a full-fledged soldier with all of your freedoms back, but you have classes with people. You're able to talk over lunch and socialize after class is over. During the weekend, your only responsibility is morning exercises with the entire unit.

We got our phones back, had access to the internet, and could even order food or go off base (with permission). But there was one major rule that marked a significant change from my previous conditions of socialization: No alcohol was allowed for anyone in AIT, even if they were off base and dressed in civilian clothing. The penalties were stiff, and I watched fellow soldiers get kicked out of the army for breaking them.

From June 4, 2013, to December 18 the same year, I was mostly sober. I had a drink once when some buddies and I went off base; we went to see *Jackass Presents: Bad Grandpa* and bought some liquor to pour into our drinks in the movie theater. Aside from that, I did not have any alcohol for six months.

The six months I spent sober in AIT were different from my

other attempts at sobriety. I didn't just stop drinking: I built a new identity fundamentally at odds with the old one in which I drank. For the first time in my adult life, I forged friendships without alcohol in the picture at all. I got to know people by talking about the books we read, the movies we watched, and our experiences in class. I took advantage of ways to connect with people I'd never tried before, like weekly Bible study and running 5ks to raise money for veterans. I even graduated at the top of my class for my MOS. More importantly, I became friends with people whom I still stay in touch with today—and I did it all without alcohol.

Attention looks like respect to those who aren't used to receiving either. While there were people who respected me because of boxing, I never noticed or cared, because I craved the approval and acceptance that I got from being liked for drinking. It's easier to be liked, but to maintain that feeling makes you more likely to do things that erode your respect. When you're respected, you stop caring who likes you—ironically, making people like you even more.

An easy way to tell the difference between attention and respect is to see how often you're invited to respectable functions. Do your friends invite you to meet their family members, or make introductions and recommendations on your behalf that could bring you money or opportunities? When people just like you for the entertainment you provide, they aren't going to attempt to get to know you beyond casual interactions. They're trying to maximize their exposure to the parts of you that they like while minimizing their exposure to your character. Put differently, if people don't respect you, they won't feel comfortable putting their reputation on the line for you, even with something as casual as a family gathering.

Alcohol has become so ingrained in our society that many people have no idea how they'll live without it. I've often wondered how many college-aged people drink because they don't know any other way to get the social connections that are a basic human desire. Everyone around them is drinking, so they drink to fit in. And I'm only speaking of my experience as someone who didn't start drinking until I was eighteen years old. The average age for the first drink in America is fifteen.

My six months away from alcohol, building a new identity and making positive connections without it, was the one thing I hadn't tried. My environment didn't allow it. No one ever forced me to drink, but I never gave my sobriety habit a chance to become strong. Once I did, it opened my eyes to a new way of living. Still, as strong as my sobriety became during my time away, old habits die hard—and it would be a different challenge to hold on to this identity once I returned to my old life.

XI

You Only Have to Get Unlucky Once to Ruin Your Life

When I got back from basic training, the first thing I wanted to do was drink. With my new identity, built around gaining self-respect and focused on accomplishing my goals, I figured I could handle myself. I'd spent six months away from my friends, gaining new skills and making progress on my life plan. I felt I deserved to party a little.

Alcohol will give you nights that you can't remember but will never forget. Here's what I can't forget: I met my friends at a bar. I was there early, already up to my old ways, drinking hard and fast to celebrate. After several drinks, I left for another bar to meet up with some more people. I'm not sure if I was tossed out or it was closing time.

I woke up at a friend's house the next day, confused about how the night had gone. And I was horrified to find that I had driven to get there. This wasn't the first time that I had driven drunk. It wasn't even the first time I couldn't remember driving that way. However, viewed through newfound clarity from my sober time during basic training, I finally felt like I had hit rock bottom.

Although no one got hurt, and I didn't get into any legal trouble, this was the first time that I felt lucky. Every other time, I just thought it was a cool story to tell people, to continue building the bullshit legend of myself. I romanticized the idea of being a heavy drinker who always had a crazy story to tell about my drinking. But now I felt like shit, and I couldn't shake the feeling that the universe was giving me one final chance to get my act together before the law of large numbers finally caught up to me.

The law of large numbers refers to the tendency for results involving randomness to stabilize or converge as more trials or instances occur. While small sample sizes show wide variation and flux, larger data sets produce results closer to the expected average. A simple example is coin flips. Flip a coin ten times, and you could get eight heads and two tails, or vice versa. The coin isn't rigged, and this probably wouldn't surprise you. But if you flip it ten thousand times, the outcome will be much closer to 50 percent heads and 50 percent tails.

So far, I had been lucky. But if I kept up my habits around alcohol, I'd have to keep getting lucky. One day, my luck would run out. My situation reminded me of what the Provisional Irish Republican Army (IRA) said in a statement to former Prime Minister Margaret Thatcher after a failed assassination attempt: "Today, we were unlucky. But remember, we only have to be lucky once—you will have to be lucky always."

I'd come so far in my life, and if I couldn't get my drinking under control, I would lose everything as soon as I was unlucky once. I was now part of the military, and their rules for a DUI were clear: I would be kicked out, with a possible dishonorable discharge. If that happened, the past six months would have been for nothing. I wouldn't be eligible for any financial aid I could use to pay for school, which was the main reason I had enlisted. A DUI would also mean that I'd lose my driver's license and my ability to get to the gym where I trained. My professional boxing career had just started, and losing my ability to drive would bring it to a screeching halt. The conviction would also make it difficult to get hired anywhere, and if I did manage to find a job, I'd have to take the bus to get there.

And then there was the relationship that I had just started. When I moved back to Pittsburgh from Los Angeles, I went on a date with the most beautiful, interesting, kind-hearted woman I'd ever met. I like to tell myself that she's lucky she met me, but I was the lucky one. I found someone who liked me for me, even when I was working at T-Mobile and only had ambitions of becoming a world-champion boxer.

I had just started seriously dating Anna. She'd even flown down to see me graduate from basic training and drove to visit me during Thanksgiving break at Fort Gregg-Adams. Our first date was at a bar. However, at the time, I just happened to be trying an alcoholic's approach to sobriety: intermittent drinking. I'd stay sober for five days while drinking myself into a stupor the other two. Our first date was on one of my sobriety days. As we continued seeing each other, I never let her see me drunk because, at that point, I knew I had a problem and it would ruin things. The future of this relationship would never get a chance to materialize if I did something dumb under the influence of alcohol one night while I was out without her.

These were just the things that would have happened if I had only been caught driving under the influence. Things would have been much worse if I hurt or killed someone. I spent all day thinking about these things, and then I did what I should have done years ago. I found the most convenient Alcoholics Anonymous meeting for me and went to it that evening.

There are mixed opinions regarding AA. Some people dislike its ideology and believe it's ineffective. Others give the organization sole credit for their double-digit years of sobriety. Regardless of one's perspective, AA has a crucial component that cannot be refuted: AA clearly identifies the culprit.

The first of AA's twelve steps is "We admitted we were powerless over alcohol and that our lives had become unmanageable." Admitting a problem comes first, and for good reason: A problem cannot be dealt with unless it is first acknowledged. If you don't think there's something wrong, you won't do anything to fix it.

I heard several stories in AA from people on their last chance. I listened to stories of people who got multiple DUIs and had mandatory AA sessions as a condition of prison release. A woman broke into tears as she shared her story about losing her children to protective services due to alcohol-related incidents.

I had two major thoughts as I digested different stories about the tumultuous paths that brought different people to the church basement. First, I thought again about how lucky I was that my relationship with alcohol hadn't led to a jail term or a tragedy. Listening to the stories of other people's misfortune made me grateful that I was getting things together before it was too late.

My second thought was *I'm not like the people here*. In retrospect, this was arrogant, but I felt like I didn't need the program. My six months away had told me everything that I needed to know: Stay away from alcohol and continue to build my identity around things not related to alcohol.

After I left the meeting, the first thing I did was type out a text message to my five closest friends:

> Hey guys. I just got out of an AA meeting. I realized that I have a problem and if I don't get it under control, I'm going to destroy myself. I understand if you don't want to hang out with me anymore, but I have to do this for myself before there's nothing left to save.

I hesitated before I hit send because I was terrified.

I feared the past because I could do nothing to fix what I'd done, mute what I had said, or erase what I'd written. People remember how an action made them feel far more than the exact details of its execution, and many people will neither forgive you nor forget what you've done, regardless of how much progress you make. I feared the future because I didn't want to return to who I was. I was worried that I lacked the willpower to stay committed to my goal. I didn't want this to be another false start I couldn't maintain or a case of regret from the night before. I thought the people I was texting would laugh at me, not take me seriously, or reject me. That kid who felt abandoned by his mother, unwanted by his father, and was always trying to gain acceptance was still a part of me. These were his fears, but I finally had the confidence to make this decision because of the man I'd become over the past six months.

I pushed through the nerves and hit send. Then I waited in the cold parking lot. I was so anxious that I forgot to turn the car's heat on in the middle of a cold, snowy December night. Then my phone buzzed.

"I love you, man. Why would I stop being friends with you?"

"You my nigga. We still good, man."

"That's more booze for me. Seriously, man, proud of you."

"Shit, you got me thinking maybe I need to take a break. We still good."

"We were friends before you started drinking. That won't stop now."

I felt a warmth surge through me. My five best friends were there for me, and that was a good feeling. But even if they had all texted back, "Fuck off, man. You were only good for drinking," it wouldn't have mattered. Just like with the moves in my boxing career and my decision to enlist in the army, I was doing this for me. Their support meant the world to me, but my goals wouldn't change even if I didn't have it.

December 23, 2013, was the first day of my new life. It was my first day of sobriety, and I was going to stick with it this time.

Idle Hands Are the Devil's Playground

I did my first year of sobriety with a cheat code—I was too busy to think about drinking, let alone have the time for it. In the first two weeks of January 2014, I enrolled in school, got a job, returned to the gym, and had my first drill with the National Guard. I didn't take on all of these activities to keep me from drinking— that was just an unintended benefit. These responsibilities were necessary to fulfill my plan and build a reality that matched my ego. But it wasn't easy.

My plan for school was to do my first four semesters at the Community College of Allegheny County (CCAC) in Pittsburgh. However, my records from when I went there after dropping out of the University of Rochester were still on file. I had failed most of my classes because I couldn't balance working and going to class. For multiple reasons, those old grades were a problem.

For the first two years, CCAC would only let me take two classes per semester, meaning I'd have to add at least another year to my plan. This pace would also disqualify me for student aid of any type because I wouldn't be a full-time student. Moreover, even if I got all As in these classes, my previous failures would still be on my transcript, and that would be a tough hurdle to overcome when applying to a four-year university to get my bachelor's degree.

Those blemishes on my early record would also almost certainly disqualify me for any scholarship, which I anticipated needing because although I would have financial assistance from the military, it wasn't the full GI Bill allotment like I'd get as an active-duty soldier. I'd still have to pay some out-of-pocket costs. At the community-college level, they'd be manageable, but at the university level, I'd need help.

To tackle this problem, I researched community colleges in surrounding counties and found that Community College of Beaver County (CCBC) offered all the courses I needed to transfer into a four-year electrical engineering program. This was ideal, since Tom's boxing gym and my fighter's camp house were both in Beaver County, and living in the same county as the college meant lower tuition costs.

With my home, gym, and school all in the same area, it made sense to find a local job, and I was fortunate to land a job at Huntington Bank's nearby Aliquippa branch. The only aspect of my life I couldn't consolidate was my military drills. This wasn't a big deal, as drills were only one weekend a month and were only a thirty-minute ride away. The drive usually took even less time than that because I'd just stay at Anna's house the weekend of drills, as her apartment was only ten minutes away. We'd be living together by the end of the year anyway, but I kept my official address in Beaver County to maintain my tuition discount.

To juggle this heavy workload, I took all required prerequisite classes first. The hustle of the American education system meant that although I planned on being an engineer, I had to take courses in English, history, microeconomics, and macroeconomics, along with a few other requirements in philosophy and literature. While I believe in being well-rounded, I hate that you're forced to pay for these classes and need them to get a degree. Fortunately for me, I could do most of these classes online.

I breezed through my mandatory classes in the spring and summer semesters. When it came time to take calculus, chemistry, physics, and programming, things became more difficult. I couldn't take those classes online, and now I had to devote more time to studying. The fights also became more challenging—but with those challenges came more opportunities.

Opportunity Brings More Opportunity

March 28, 2014, was my first fight after enlisting and starting school. Rubin Williams was once a highly touted contender who had challenged for the IBF super middleweight title in 2005. Although he lost, he'd won a few minor titles against good fighters and was featured on the boxing reality TV show *The Contender*. By the time we fought, though, his best days were far behind him.

He'd lost his last twenty-one fights, with eleven losses coming by knockout. His record was a dismal 29–23–1. At that point in his career, he was just a warm body who showed up for a paycheck— and the check wasn't even that great. He took my fight on a day's notice because he needed the six hundred dollars for groceries. He needed the money so badly that he only arrived at the venue thirty minutes before our fight because his car broke down on the way there.

When the ring announcer introduces the fighters, he normally mentions their record, but when a fighter has a record with as many losses as Williams, he just says, "A veteran of over fifty fights." I dismantled him in under a minute in the first round, but this was hardly impressive. Rubin didn't even train anymore; he just sacrificed his body for less than he'd make working part-time, earning minimum wage. After nine more fights, all of which he lost by knockout, he laid himself completely to rest in the Fighter's Graveyard and retired.

My next fight was on May 7 against Travis Fulton. Fulton was famous in the mixed martial arts community, holding the record for the most MMA fights in history. He was another fighter who would take a fight on short notice for a paycheck, but unlike Rubin Williams, Fulton avoided getting knocked out at all costs. When a fighter is knocked out, he's usually suspended by the state's athletic commission for thirty to ninety days. While the suspension is good for the fighter's health, it's bad for his bank account. Time suspended means that a fighter can't fight in that state, and many states, though not required to, honor other states' suspensions.

When we fought, Fulton's record was 21–36–1. I dropped him in the first round with my best punch—a left hook from hell. He barely beat the count but wouldn't risk getting knocked out after that. He took every chance he got to hold me. After two warnings and three point deductions, he was disqualified, and my professional record moved to 5–0.

When I finished the summer semester at school, I was at a crossroads. I had completed all of the mandatory prerequisite classes; I could finally start taking the classes that mattered. But to do this, I'd have to stop working at the bank. As a member of the National Guard, while I wasn't eligible for the GI Bill, I could receive federal tuition assistance of $250 per semester hour if I was enrolled at an approved school. But BCCC was not on the list. Meanwhile, my cost-of-living allowance, by itself, wasn't enough to replace what I made at the bank.

I did the math. With my drill pay, National Guard assistance, and cost-of-living allowance, I could survive the fall semester if I got at least one fight before it ended. Although my purse depended solely upon how many tickets I sold, I hadn't yet made anything less than five hundred dollars from a fight. Things would be tight, but I could pull it off if I didn't get any surprise bills. I put in my two weeks' notice at the bank at the beginning of August. In September 2014, I started a full in-person schedule of calculus, chemistry, physics, electronics, and C++ programming.

No fights were on the horizon, but I spent four to five hours in the gym every day after class. The nature of professional fighting is that you never know when you'll get a call to be a last-minute replacement on a show. Even if you aren't called to fill in on a major show that could be your next big break, every win gets a fighter closer to signing with a promoter and making bigger, more consistent paydays.

Except for Fulton's disqualification, I had won all of my fights by knockout. As a result, even guys with losing records wanted more money than my ability to sell tickets to cover their purses. I already wasn't selling enough tickets to fully cover the cost of my opponents. I only got the fights I did because one of the fighters who passed through AAH was Angelo Magnone, a former defensive end from Bowling Green State University.

After being cut from the program, Angelo had returned home to Steubenville, Ohio, and used his experience in California to build Made Men Promotions. He put me on shows even though I was a net profit loss, partly out of generosity but primarily because he hoped that I'd sign with him so he could sell my contract to a bigger promoter after I got a few wins. But the cost of my opponents was starting to exceed his generosity. To continue fighting, I had three options: take a tough fight I was most likely to lose and learn nothing from, get signed with a promoter, or get a financial backer.

As a pro fighter riding high with five victories and no losses, I thought I could beat anyone, but Tom had a different idea. "It's like a boat in the ocean trying to get to land, but there's a hurricane between it and the shore. So, the boat's got two choices: Go through the hurricane or go around it. We're trying to go around the storm, not through it." In this metaphor, my career was the boat, and the shore was a big payday or championship. There were two ways to get there: taking tough opponents against whom I was the major underdog, or getting someone to invest in my career and taking fights that were challenging enough to develop my skills, but not so much that I had only a small chance of winning.

"But ain't going around the storm longer?"

"You ever drive in a rainstorm? Ain't nobody driving fast when they can't see. And besides, if you take a little boat through a big hurricane, it's gonna get broken to pieces, and everyone's gonna drown."

"Makes sense," I said. Tom's point was clear: Even though the path through the hurricane was a straight line, it was a journey most guys never completed.

"Now, if you gotta go through the storm, you gotta go through the storm," Tom concluded. "Some guys ain't good sailors and got a shitty sense of direction. But if you got a good captain, he ain't gonna take you through the hurricane unless there's no choice."

Most guys in my situation who don't have competent management or coaching choose the first option: They build an undefeated record against subpar opposition before being fed to a fighter with a similar record but with proper training and management. As a fighter, you're supposed to believe you can beat everyone, but your coach and manager are there to protect you from yourself. They're the captains of the ship, with the knowledge of the best routes and the ability and experience to safely navigate them. I was fortunate that I had Tom as my coach, and his brother Mark as my manager, to keep me from going straight through the storm. And, even if I had wanted to, the record-building only works if guys are willing to get in the ring with you.

Mark Yankello had built an impressive list of connections over his twenty years of working on fights with his brother. Even in the age of social media and publicly available email addresses, boxing connections are facilitated by in-person interactions. The more people you know, the more people you get to know—and Mark knew a lot of people. In September 2014, we got the interest of a potential financial backer named David McWater.

The way financial backing works in boxing is like venture capital. A backer invests into covering the costs of developing a fighter he thinks has great potential. In exchange, the fighter gives up a percentage of his future earnings when he starts getting bigger paydays. It's a simple system, but it's not ideal. Signing a promotional agreement with a major promoter is the best path forward for a fighter, but those deals are hard to get. The financial backer helps you get there by doing things like paying fighters enough to make risking brain damage worth it. Should a fighter sign a big deal with a major promoter after getting financial backing, the backer still gets a piece of that.

Like venture capitalists, a financial backer needs to have enough money to not worry about his investment failing. McWater had made his fortune from selling a couple of bars he owned in Manhattan and playing in high-stakes poker games at the infamous Mayfair Club. Before McWater would invest in me, he wanted to see me in action. On October 2, Tom, Mark, and I drove up to the Mohegan Sun casino in Connecticut for a fight against Excell Holmes.

Holmes had a losing record, but he put up some resistance. I quickly overwhelmed him and scored a first-round knockout. This was the first fight around which I had to manage conflicts with my class schedule—I had to take a chemistry exam two days before the rest of the class because I would miss the test for my fight.

Despite a stellar performance that made him want to sign me, in the end I didn't go with McWater, because Mark used the footage of the fight to attract the attention of a new boxing promoter: Roc Nation Sports.

Never Forget the People Who Were There for You When You Needed Them Most

Rap mogul Jay-Z started Roc Nation as a record label in 2008. In 2013, he expanded into sports management by founding Roc Nation Sports under the same corporate umbrella. Initially, the outfit focused only on sports played with a ball, but they eventually decided to try boxing.

Mark negotiated the deal, and in April 2015, Roc Nation Sports officially became my boxing promoter. This meant that I'd no longer have to expend energy selling tickets; I would also make at least $4,000 per fight and receive a monthly stipend of $1,000. For comparison, the most money I had made selling tickets up to that point was $792—and that took almost as much time as training for the fight!

The idea of being associated with Roc Nation Sports was exciting. Only boxing fans knew the names of the big boxing promoters, but everyone knew who Jay-Z was and knew of his company, Roc Nation. If something like this had happened to me a few years before, I'd have celebrated by drinking myself into a stupor, but now I was approaching two years of sobriety, and I had no desire to drink ever again.

When I first got sober, I nearly had to trick myself into sticking with it. When I craved a drink in the little spaces of downtime I had, I told myself that I could drink after I wrote a book, won a boxing title, or graduated from school. That was my way of dealing with the desire to relapse. I didn't know it at the time, but I was negotiating my way through agony, the same way that you tell yourself that if you can make it through something painful, it'll be worth it. That's what I was doing with booze—but after a year and a half of sobriety, I knew I'd never go back.

If I had a little bit of free time to entertain the idea of drinking before, I didn't have it in 2015. That summer, I graduated from CCBC and transferred to Duquesne University to finish my degree. My ambitions had changed, and I was now pursuing a degree in physics rather than electrical engineering. While there are no jobs solely titled "physicist" like there are for "electrical engineer," it was a heavily math-based degree that appeared to be more flexible and presented more options than an engineering track. Plus, I just enjoyed studying it.

I fought four times in 2015. My last fight of the year took place on December 11, at the Wellsburg fire hall in Wellsburg, West Virginia. Most people don't realize that in boxing there is no such thing as a dedicated structure, like a "boxing stadium" or "boxing field," the way there is for other sports. The only thing you need to put on a state-sanctioned fight is two willing combatants and a place with enough space, cheap enough to rent, that fits enough people to make a profit selling tickets while staying under the occupancy limit. The Wellsburg fire hall served our purposes.

The fighters were supposed to warm up in one building, then walk across a cold, snowy parking lot to enter the fight venue. Tom had cornered many fights in his career, and even he was surprised by this setup. So, he ignored the rules and cleared out a space in the corner of the standing-room-only hall where the fights were to take place. As we warmed up, the crowds got drunker and rowdier. Some gathered around to watch me warm up and even tried to talk to us, but we just ignored them and stayed focused.

That night, I would face the six-foot-four, 240-pound Terrell Jamal Woods. He was 19–4 as an amateur but had a rough start when he turned pro. He lost his first fight by a questionable referee stoppage, giving his opponent a technical knockout (TKO) victory. Still, he'd never even been knocked down in a fight, let alone properly knocked out. When we met, his record was 8–23–4. At first glance, that record seemed worse than any of the guys I'd fought before. However, a closer look at his record made it clear that this guy was not to be taken lightly.

All eight of his victories had come by way of knockout—and not technical knockouts, where the referee makes the decision based on your inability or unwillingness to continue fighting. He was putting guys to sleep. Of his twenty-three losses, only four came by technical knockout. After his first loss, he had no chance of getting a manager or promoter, so he became a journeyman, able to fight ten to twelve times a year because he never got hurt. Big-time promoters use guys like Woods to test their fighters, to ensure they're progressing and ready for bigger, televised fights. This is exactly what Roc Nation was doing to me.

"Don't let this guy's record deceive you," Tom told me. "He's a big, strong kid who got home-cooked and robbed a few times. He can hurt you if you don't stick to the game plan and fight your ass off." Getting "robbed" in a fight happens when the judges' scorecards give the win to the guy who clearly lost. When it happens in front of a crowd full of the actual loser's fans, we call it "home cooking," because it usually goes down in the guy's hometown—a sweet little gift for the local hero, just like momma's home-cooked meal.

For this fight, I kept things simple. I kept my opponent busy defending against my jab, snapping it out with an unpredictable rhythm and occasionally switching it up to a hook that landed square on his jaw. In the second round, that hook knocked him off-balance, forcing him to clinch just to stay upright. But no matter what, I couldn't get him down. I'd toss in a right cross after the jab to keep him guessing, all the while making sure I didn't get countered by his devastating right hand.

My plan was to keep him so worried about my punches that he wouldn't have time to launch his own attack. I shut down his offense by keeping him on edge, reminding him with every punch that I had the power and skill to hurt him—something he wouldn't forget after tasting that hook in the second round.

In the corner before the final round, Tom gave me another warning.

"When you hear the sound for ten seconds remaining, this guy's gonna let everything fly. That's how he won the last fight. He was down on the scorecards going into the last round, and he just went for broke."

I was controlling the entire final round. When the three clacks came from the timekeeper, alerting everyone that only ten seconds remained in the bout, sure enough, Woods's aggression went into overdrive. He caught me with a hook that buckled my knees, but it was just as the bell rang. That flurry of activity won him that round on all the judges' cards, but he still lost a unanimous decision.

I was now 10–0 as a professional heavyweight boxer. This victory was a great way to end 2015 and bring in the new year. To celebrate, I used part of my four-thousand-dollar prize money to buy a Christmas gift for each friend I had texted when I got out of my first AA meeting two years earlier. They were my friends before I started drinking and while I was at my lowest points, and they'd remained my biggest supporters in sobriety.

The Better the Opposition, the Better You Must Become to Move Past It

After my win over Jamal Woods, I started to fight guys with better skills and winning records. Now I had to spend more time training, which required more recovery time. Everyone understands that the life of a professional fighter is physically exhausting, but people rarely think about the mental and emotional energy that goes into the lifestyle.

In April 2016, I fought Hassan Lee. His record was 5–4, and he was the first guy I'd fought with a winning record since my professional debut against Jon Hill. At six foot five, he was my tallest professional opponent yet, but I'd beaten taller guys as an amateur while at All-American Heavyweights.

Lee fought me exactly as I expected someone with a four-inch height advantage would. He tried to keep me at a distance with his jab, but he wasn't fast enough to make contact. I would simply

HARD LESSONS FROM THE HURT BUSINESS

slip inside and pummel his midsection with punches to the heart, liver, and stomach. Those punches aren't as flashy, but they are destructive. When you get hit with a disruptive headshot, your nervous system is scrambled. Many times, the unfortunate recipient of a headshot doesn't even remember getting hit. He just wakes up on the canvas and doesn't even feel the pain until the next day. However, body shots sap the fighter's energy, force him to breathe harder, and are incredibly painful.

After eating a few of those body shots, Lee started to drop his hands to his sides after each jab in an attempt to keep me from tenderizing his ribs. That left him open for a powerful right cross over the top that dropped him in the second round. He got to his feet and continued the bout, but that punch completely robbed him of his will to fight. He survived the next round by holding me whenever I got close, but that tactic sapped his energy. When I dropped him again in the fourth round, he didn't rise to his feet before the referee counted to eight.

That July, I fought Juan Goode. It was the first time I fought in Pittsburgh since winning the Pennsylvania Golden Gloves tournament in March 2011. The fight was held outside, behind the Rivers Casino, in a beautiful area along the Ohio River. I spent the week of the fight obsessing over the weather forecast, as there was a small chance of storms, but fortunately we had a clear night for the fight.

Goode's record was 6–3, with five of those wins coming by way of knockout. He'd also had an impressive amateur boxing career, which included a Michigan Golden Gloves title and a third-place finish at the 2010 national men's tournament. His professional record and amateur accolades were clear indicators of his skill, but the even bigger problem was one that I hadn't encountered before: his weight.

Goode weighed in for our fight at 250 pounds, while I tipped the scales at 220. I was used to being the shorter fighter, but I had never been outweighed by so much. At six foot one, Goode was the same height as me, but the extra weight meant his punches would land with a lot more momentum. If you saw him on the street and didn't know that he was an accomplished boxer, you would think he was overweight and out of shape. When I first saw him, I thought that as well. I imagined that the extra weight combined with fighting in the hot, humid July air would have him gasping for air by the second round. This was a gross miscalculation.

By the end of the first round, I knew why he'd had the success that he did. He was a smart, strong, surprisingly well-conditioned fighter. Not only were his punches accurate, but he was adept at putting the weight of his entire body behind each shot. His jabs rattled me almost as much as power punches. Every time I got a little lazy with my punches, he countered. I had gotten so used to fighting opponents taller than me that I had trouble adjusting to someone my own height.

Between every round, Tom would tell me either, "All right—you lost that round," or, "OK—you won that round. Keep doing that and stay on his ass, because this one is close, and we don't know how the judges will see it." I won my twelfth professional fight in the most brutal split decision possible. Two of the three judges saw me winning four of the six rounds, with the third judge giving the fight to Goode by a score of 5–1.

A few days later, the mother of my friend who watched the fight said to me, "Are you all right? You got hit a lot in that fight!" I had lingering headaches and dizzy spells, but that's par for the course as a professional boxer. I was hit more than usual in that fight, and it was the first professional bout that I did not win convincingly.

I didn't have much time to recover from that fight before I learned I would be the opening fight on Showtime on September 23, two months away. The fight would be shown worldwide, and my opponent would be the son of a legendary champion.

XII

Old Endings
Are New Beginnings

You ever see *The Hunger Games*?" I asked Tom after finishing the press conference with the other fighters ahead of the biggest fight of my life. Tom shook his head. I should have known better than to ask him: If it wasn't related to boxing, Tom didn't even know it existed.

"Oh, yeah, I watched that with my daughter," Mark chimed in. "That's the one where they make all the kids fight to death for everyone to watch?"

"Yeah, man. This is just like that. All this pageantry and these interviews before they watch us try to kill each other—and if it wasn't for the ref, we'd do exactly that."

"Well, you better fuckin' try to kill him," Tom said. "You win this, and your stock is gonna go way up." He'd been telling me all week that beating Trey Lippe Morrison would get the press talking, boost demand for me, and put me in a position to make real money.

All of the interviews and photo shoots I went through in the days before the fight were meant to get the word out. The clash between Trey Lippe Morrison, the son of former World Boxing Association heavyweight boxing champion Tommy Morrison, and Ed Latimore, an amateur national champion pursuing a physics degree, was so interesting that it made the front page of *USA Today*'s sports section. In the final two weeks leading up to the fight, I spent more time giving interviews than training. Roc Nation was promoting the fight. The Showtime network was promoting the fight.

I was finally on the big stage.

Despite Trey Lippe Morrison's lineage, he was inexperienced, having only been fighting for three years. But he was tough, and he had incredible punching power: So far, he'd won every fight by knockout. Of the three years he'd been boxing, he'd spent one year nursing a broken right hand back to life. That's how hard he hit—he punched another professional boxer in the face, knocked him out cold, and, in the process, broke his own hand.

Boxing analysts expected our fight to be competitive, but most considered me the favorite. After all, I was also undefeated. Between my amateur and professional careers, I had ten years of experience, seventy fights, a victory over an Olympian, and a national amateur title. Trey Lippe Morrison had no amateur experience; our fight was only his twelfth.

The fight occurred in Miami, Oklahoma, not to be confused with the more well-known Miami, Florida. As you know, Miami,

Florida, is a bustling, Latin-infused coastal city of nearly half a million residents, attracting over fifty million visitors and tourists yearly. Miami, Oklahoma, is an old mining town by an Indian reservation an hour northeast of Tulsa.

Eventually, all the pageantry and grandstanding ended, and the day of the actual fight arrived. I felt the hostility radiating from the crowd when the announcer called my name and I began walking to the ring. Trey was from Tulsa, so there was a home-field advantage for him. As soon as I entered the arena for my ring walk, a chorus of boos erupted that grew more intense the closer I got to taking center stage. I stepped through the ropes, took a deep breath, and soaked it all in. I enjoyed having the odds stacked against me.

Once Trey started walking to the ring, the hometown crowd erupted. At that moment, in true stoic fashion, I detached myself from the moment and focused inward. I remembered that I was there to fight—to do a job. That was all.

We met in the center of the ring, and the referee gave the usual spiel. "You got your instructions in the dressing room. Any questions?"

Trey shook his head.

"Any questions?"

I shook my head.

Once the fight got going, I was doing well. I was throwing punches, moving, and hitting my opponent without getting hit. I was taking advantage of his inexperience. And then I misplaced my footing, and I slipped. Well, I thought I slipped.

I wouldn't realize until I watched the fight a few months later that I didn't slip. Morrison threw a shot so fast that I didn't see it coming and so powerful that it didn't hurt. The impact disrupted my nervous system, so my legs gave out almost instantly. I got demolished by a right hand that arrived at a perfect angle around my guard.

The Punch You Don't See Is the One That Does the Most Damage

They always say that it's the punch you don't see that does the most damage. I had always intellectually understood this, but now I had a visceral experience with it. In my ten years of boxing, no one had ever hit me so hard and unexpectedly as Trey Lippe Morrison hit me.

Casual and even serious boxing fans typically misunderstand, underappreciate, or are unaware of this aspect of professional prizefighting. Only those who have competed at the amateur and professional levels can appreciate the destructive power of a ten-ounce glove that fits around the padding and effectively functions as a plaster cast. To help you understand why a gloved fist causes greater damage than a bare one, let me give you a short lesson in boxing and physics.

Boxers compete with gloves. It's commonly thought that these gloves soften the blows and enhance fighter safety, and intuitively, this is a reasonable assumption. A cushion should lessen the impact of the collision between two objects: in this case, the fighter's fist and whichever unfortunate soul is on the receiving end.

This is, in fact, how the gloves work in amateur boxing competitions. The gloves used in those fights have most of their weight allocated in the fist. Whatever material is used for the padding primarily comprises the weight of a boxing glove. In the case of amateur boxing, that material is either latex or injection-molded foam that gives quite a bit during impact. This design, and the padded head protection required for amateur boxing competitions, is why it is rare to see an amateur fighter get knocked out.

Professional gloves, however, are designed to maximize force transmission, with padding in the wrist and just enough around the fist to protect the knuckles. Often made with materials like horsehair, professional gloves provide less cushion, allowing fighters to hit harder and cause more damage. When a punch lands in a professional glove, there is less give, and the fighter can hit harder and with more destructive power than he could with his fist alone.

I tell you all of this because I want you to understand just how hard I got hit that night. After that crushing overhand right dropped me to the canvas, I quickly sprang to my feet. While I had to rise to my feet before the referee's count reached ten, no rule said I had to get up as quickly as possible. I should have used more of the count to recover better, but I wanted to show everyone that I wasn't hurt. Remember, I thought that I had slipped.

"Are you OK?" the referee asked. He has to ask this, but he doesn't care. In the boxing ring, you have no friends—there's just your opponent and the referee, who ensures the fight follows the Marquess of Queensberry rules.

"Do you want to continue?" he said after my nod. Of course, I wanted to continue, but this is another question that the referee has to ask. He made me take two steps forward, to ensure I could fight, and then he stepped out of the way for the contest to continue.

I was rattled but still aware—or so I thought. I advanced, and I "slipped" again. This time, I felt it. I got cracked and dropped again while up against the ropes. I got back up again and the ref looked into my eyes. He saw something he didn't like, which prompted him to wave his hands over his head to signal the end of the contest.

I lost in the most embarrassing way possible—a first-round technical knockout. According to the judges' official scorecard, it only took one minute and fifty-three seconds.

"If the Worst Thing That Happens to You Is Losing a Fight, Life Is Good."

Life is not what happens to us. Life is how we perceive what happens to us and around us. How we see those events determines how we'll react to them, and our reactions determine the quality of our lives. I'd been practicing this Stoic philosophy since I was a child, but I didn't really understand it until I got beaten in the ring.

The morning after the fight, I did not want to interact with society on any level. I didn't check my phone or social media, and I delayed heading downstairs for breakfast as long as possible.

Twenty-four hours earlier, my ego was riding high, knowing

I'd be on cable television. I had obnoxiously texted everyone in my phone photos and updates of the event, to the point where at least three people blocked me. Now, I just wanted to be left alone to lick my wounds and nurse my battered ego, but I couldn't stay in my hotel room forever.

I was also physically hurting, now that the adrenaline of the event had worn off. I had not felt this bad waking up since the morning of my first full day of sobriety. To say I was depressed is probably too strong, but I felt awful and was full of self-pity.

The hotel didn't care about my self-pity. Checkout was at 11:00 a.m., and I had to get something to eat ahead of a long day of flying back home. I wandered down to the lobby, where the other fighters were eating breakfast. I grabbed some bacon, eggs, and one of those waffles made by squeezing the batter into the cup and pouring it into the rotating waffle iron. I love those waffles, so having one raised my spirits slightly—the first reminder that maybe life wasn't so bad. I sat by myself and enjoyed my meal, hoping I wouldn't be bothered by anyone who might want to talk about the fight.

Usually, I'd be checking social media while eating breakfast, but I had turned my phone off because I still wasn't ready to face the outside world and deal with the shame of my loss. I didn't want to see anything about the fight, because the internet is forever, but more importantly, the internet is fast. I was probably the star of at least a hundred memes at this point. So, I did something unusual for me: I started watching the news on the television in the hotel lobby.

I try to avoid news of domestic and international politics. This is also in accordance with my Stoic philosophy: I can't do anything about these events, so I don't worry about them. The news almost exclusively discusses negative, politically charged, socially divisive topics in the most polarizing way possible. If something is really important, I won't be able to ignore it anyway.

But that morning, I learned about the bombings in Aleppo, Syria. I learned how the bombings affected the people there. Images of what remained of the city flashed on the screen, reminding me of a post-apocalyptic war zone—because the bombings left that city exactly like that.

The next news story was about a police shooting that had just occurred in Charlotte, North Carolina. The shooting of Keith Lamont Scott had taken place on September 20, but I was so busy with my preparation for the fight that I'd had no idea. The news outlets were running that story as a comparison to the police shooting of Terence Crutcher in Tulsa earlier that month.

The last story that aired that morning told of a tragic event that had taken place the night before, while I was in the midst of the fight. A twenty-year-old psycho by the name of Arcan Cetin had walked into the Cascade Mall in Washington State and shot five people dead, one of whom was a sixteen-year-old cancer survivor.

After seeing those three news stories, a wave of sadness washed away the despair that had distorted my perspective. I had just lost a fight on broadcast television in the most humiliating way possible. The loss shattered my ego, robbed me of my ability to earn money, and embarrassed me in front of the world. But all three news stories drove home a different, brutal reality: I could still go home to my loved ones. Many others in the world weren't so lucky.

I could give up boxing and do something else with my life, or get back in the ring and keep pushing. Either way, I had something that the people in those news stories no longer had: a choice. They had lost their lives for no other reason than they were in the wrong place at the wrong time.

When I was preparing for the Olympic trials in California, All-American Heavyweights got UFC legend and action-film star Randy Couture to speak to us. We asked him about his life in the Octagon, his time filming *The Expendables*, and how he dealt with success and failure.

On dealing with his failures, he said something that stuck with me. I've shared this wisdom with other fighters who have lost and are going through the emotional downswing that happens after coming out on the wrong end of an ass-kicking.

"If the worst thing that happens to you is losing a fight, life is good."

Relationships Are the Most Important Thing in Life

When I returned to Pittsburgh from Miami, a FedEx express letter from Roc Nation Sports had already been delivered, officially releasing me from my contract and wishing me the best of luck. My showing was so bad that they fired me before I could even make it home.

To be honest, after I had my epiphany over breakfast, I didn't mind losing. Losing by a first-round knockout on international television sucked, but I knew that people had other things to worry about. Most people didn't watch the fight, and even the ones who did had more pressing concerns. I was a temporary entertainment. I was out of their mind faster than I had lost. So, losing wasn't my main concern. My problem was far more immediate: money.

I got $8,500 for my fight. After I paid my trainer and manager, paid back a loan, and put away money for taxes, I had $4,000 left—enough to cover my living expenses for, at most, three months. I planned to return to school for the spring 2017 semester, but I was no longer in the military, so I wouldn't get any extra money to cover my cost of living.

I had bet on myself, but this time, unlike when I was training for the Golden Gloves tournament, I came up short. In response, I did the only thing I knew how to do at this point in my life: I started looking for a job. Unlike after I got cut from All-American Heavyweights, I now had a litany of credentials: an associate's degree in engineering, a transcript of physics classes, real experience troubleshooting and repairing electronic equipment, and military service.

The bad news was that everyone who wanted to hire me insisted I drop out of college and work full-time. But that was never an option for me—I was too close to finishing my degree, with too much time, money, and energy already invested. Besides, I had planned to take 2017 off from boxing to recover and complete my degree before getting back in the ring. One loss wouldn't keep me from fighting, but I needed to let my body heal and finish what I had started. So, I turned down those well-paying jobs and focused on finding something that would let me keep going to school.

I got a job delivering packages for a company that did outsourcing for Amazon. I had to be there by 5:00 a.m. and deliver on my route until 5:00 p.m. Winter was setting in, so it was cold and brutal. Lunch breaks were legally required, but it was impossible to make all your deliveries if you took one. But the job paid $150 per day, and the boss said he'd work with my schedule when I returned to school. It wasn't the best situation, but I could handle difficult work, and it allowed for a more manageable lifestyle than working overnight.

My delivery van malfunctioned the Tuesday before Thanksgiving. While parked on an incline, the transmission failed, and it rolled down the hill. I almost got caught underneath it but jumped out of the way at the last minute. Instead, it ran into a family's yard and garage.

The company didn't care about me or even the van. They needed to make their bottom line, so they sent another van out to pick me up and transport the packages, and I continued my route with another driver. The other driver complained about the job for the entire day. The whole experience was enough for me to quit and take my chances looking for something better. I didn't even put in my two weeks' notice. I had to find another way to make a living.

I looked for paid internships, but not having been in school for the previous semester meant they were all filled by the time I went looking. Eventually, I found a gig: A hotel wanted me to work on their accounting. The only problem was that the job was over-night, but this wouldn't be a problem. I excitedly told Anna the news.

"So, it's overnight, for three days of the week? How will you manage school, and when are you going to be awake to spend time with me?"

She was right. Life isn't only about making money; you have to nurture your relationships. Otherwise, what's the point? If I were working nights and finishing my last two semesters for my physics degree, I wouldn't have time for the most important person in my life, who had supported my personal and professional goals so far—and I felt like I owed a lot of my new life to her.

"I think you're better than that and can find something better," she said. I didn't believe her, but I trusted her faith in me.

I found work as a tutor through the website Varsity Tutors. While it paid more per hour than the delivery job, the work was inconsistent. Some weeks I'd have ten hours of work, while other weeks I got only two hours, and because of how far away the students I worked with were, most of that money was eaten up by gas. The work was interesting, but not looking at any math for over six months had made me rusty and created some embarrass-ing situations. On Election Night, I met a student in the Univer-sity of Pittsburgh's Hillman Library, and I couldn't help him solve any of the problems he had paid for help with. The student was understandably pissed and left me a terrible review, and from that point on, I didn't get any more assignments from the website.

Anna's belief that I could do better was still just a belief. I needed it to become a reality.

Sometimes the Best Move Is to Not Move

Under the terms of my fight negotiations with Trey Morrison, his promoters had guaranteed me another fight at the Buffalo Run Casino, in Oklahoma, regardless of my status with Roc Nation Sports. Mark suggested taking another fight in the meantime, because if I suffered two consecutive losses, I'd be relegated to the role of a journeyman, taking fights in which I'd be the massive underdog just to stay in the boxing game.

The fight was against Willis Lockett, a guy I had beaten before. The idea was to get me an easy win to rebuild my confidence, but training for that fight was miserable. I was still dealing with the lingering effects of the concussion from getting knocked out. I would make only five hundred dollars—fifty-five of which would go to my trainer—for the fight. I was also stressed out, worrying about my dwindling cash supply with no income source in sight.

The gym had gone from a place where I blocked out everything else to work on my craft to a painful reminder of how bad things had become. I didn't want to be there, but I felt like I didn't have a choice.

"What are you doing for money now?" Tom asked at the end of another training session I had forced myself through. Tom knew that my only income source had been the payments from Roc Nation, and he was curious how I was getting by.

"I took a job that almost got me killed. Now I tutor high school students through—"

"Almost killed you?!"

I told him the story about the van that almost flattened me, the complaining coworker, and how I quit to look for something better.

"Now I tutor high school students through a site called Varsity Tutors. There's not a lot of work, but I do what I can."

Tom went silent for a few seconds.

"Lemme talk to my wife. She's always talking about how they need tutors. Gimme a few days."

I didn't expect anything from it, but it was a nice gesture. A few days later, I had my fight with Lockett. Either he had gotten better or I had gotten worse. In our first fight, in Detroit, I nearly decapitated him with a left hook in the first round. That fight should have been stopped, but the ref gave him a long count. I cruised on to win a majority decision.

In our rematch, in West Virgina, I couldn't land anything significant. Not only that, but he was pushing me around and easily hitting me with punches that I could see coming, but my reflexes were on ice. My fight with Lockett ended in a draw. It was better than a loss, but Tom and another coach who had been watching me fight since my amateur days both noticed the degradation of my physical skills.

For me, it was clear sign that I needed to step away from boxing, maybe even permanently.

"Hey, Mark," I said afterward. "Tell the people down in Oklahoma to not worry about the fight."

"I think you'll be fine," he replied. "A draw ain't the best outcome, but it's not a loss."

"Yeah, but I'm taking time off. I need it."

"Shit, you saw his legs," Tom chimed in. "He's beat-up. The gym will be here if and whenever you're ready."

The truth was, I needed to finally deal with the other areas of my life. I'd spent the last three years in a constant state of mental, physical, and emotional exhaustion. I was sleep-deprived and out of money, and my body was collapsing.

It was time for a break.

Being Good at Something Keeps You from Discovering What You're Great At

"So, I just got off the phone with Mya's mom. She's really excited and thinks you'll do a great job with their daughter."

Tom's wife was a counselor at Mars Area High School, in the suburbs of Pittsburgh. She told me she'd see what she could do about getting me a job tutoring the students there, and she came through just in time. By the start of 2017, the only source of income I'd had since surviving the delivery van mishap was from someone who reached out to me for mindset coaching.

In February that year, I had also self-published my first book, *Not Caring What Other People Think Is a Superpower: Insights from a Heavyweight Boxer.* I now had more than eleven thousand followers on Twitter and three thousand subscribers to my newsletter, and my website was getting a few hundred visitors a day. Promoting my book through these channels brought in a few hundred dollars per month. It wasn't enough to live on, but this money was keeping me above water while I kept looking for other opportunities.

Now Tom's wife had come through with a tutoring job, and I was elated to have another source of income. The best part was that the hours worked perfectly, because my classes ended at 2:00 p.m., and Mya, the student I'd be tutoring, didn't leave school until 3:00.

After my success helping Mya, word spread to other parents whose children were struggling with math and physics. Parents from other schools heard about my results and wanted their children to work with me. Within a month of working with the first student, I had to raise my rates to slow down requests. When that didn't work, I had to start turning down work. I had stumbled into the perfect gap.

Anyone with the math and science skills to tutor high schoolers has a well-paying, demanding job available. Usually, those with the communication skills to be a good teacher don't also have quantitative skills. There was high demand and low supply, and best of all, I genuinely enjoyed the work. If you had told me, a failing student in all math disciplines in high school, that in a few years I'd be helping people prepare for the AP Physics and AP Calculus exams, I would have laughed at you. But this is exactly what happened. It all started because I believed in going back to the foundations and building things up from there.

At the start of the fall semester in 2017, things were humming along. My body had recovered from the incessant beatings and nonstop training routine and the damage done to it from basic training and from my amateur boxing career. I was making a great living tutoring in the evenings and on the weekends, and I was genuinely at peace. The only thing left to conquer was my degree.

I wanted to finish school as quickly as possible, mainly because I was running out of financial aid. I also planned to start my training again at the start of 2018, and it would have been excellent to have only boxing to focus on. I'd likely keep tutoring because I was in such high demand that even charging sixty dollars an hour hadn't put a dent in the inquiries I got. It only made my existing clients want to lock me down for more hours so they wouldn't risk losing me to another family.

I was on pace to graduate in May 2018; I had only thirteen credits of 400-level physics classes remaining before graduating. I thought it would be a brilliant idea to take solid-state physics, thermodynamics, electricity and magnetism, and mechanics all in the same semester. This workload was so intense that the school required your academic adviser to sign off on it. I presented my plan to Dr. Frittelli, my adviser, and she signed off so quickly that it gave me an extra boost of confidence. If the head of the physics department thought I could do it, maybe I had been underestimating what I could do this entire time.

It turned out, though, that this level of work nearly destroyed me, because I simply didn't have time to learn it all properly. In addition to this workload, I started the semester by moving to a new apartment, and I was on a deadline for a freelance writing project. I was also meeting tutoring clients every evening of the week. The combination of these factors made it impossible for me to do well. By midterms, I was failing every course. My professors wondered what was going on with me, as they knew my work ethic was better than this. When midterm reports came out, I realized that even though I wanted to be done with school after this semester, I needed to reduce my class load to give me a chance to pass.

To withdraw, I also needed my adviser's approval.

"Hey, Dr. Frittelli. This was a bad idea. I need to withdraw from thermodynamics and solid-state physics. I'm dying tryin' to keep up. I know you saw the midterm report."

She smiled and began speaking in her thick Argentinian accent. "Well, when you told me your plan to take these four classes, I thought it was a bad idea. But I also knew that if I told you that, you wouldn't listen to me anyway. Plus, I like to help people if their plans aren't too outrageous."

With that, she signed off on my withdrawal slip, and I was free from a heavy burden. I'd have to come back for another semester, and I still had a lot of work to do to pass the classes I hadn't withdrawn from, but now it was possible.

I spent the remainder of the fall semester recovering my failing grades in mechanics and electromagnetism, eking out a C in both classes. It was not stellar, but I wouldn't have to retake any classes. I was back on pace to graduate the following spring.

Quit While You're Ahead or Risk Falling Back Worse Than Where You Started

True to my plan, I started training again in 2018. I eased my way back into the gym, going three evenings a week and Saturdays so I still had time to tutor. I didn't need to tutor nearly as much because my rates were high. My self-published book was selling well, and I started affiliate marketing using my website and large social media presence to drive sales.

This time, I wasn't going back to boxing for money or fame. I was there to develop mastery and see how good I could become. After a few months in the gym, word got out that I was back, and a New Zealand–based promoter offered me an August fight against Junior Pati, a New Zealander who had become a fan of my social media content. He wanted to fight me before retiring. I just wanted to get back into the ring, but to get a trip to New Zealand out of it was an unexpected perk.

Although I had been back in the gym since January, I hadn't gotten in any sparring. It was difficult to find sparring, and I was eager to test my ability, so without telling my coach, I drove four hours to Toledo, Ohio, for a two-day sparring session against an old sparring partner, Cassius Anderson.

If I'd told Tom, he would've warned me it was a bad idea— after all, I'd been out for seventeen months, while Cassius had been training nonstop. I was strong and healthy, but my timing wasn't there yet. Tom would've told me that if I'd gone to him, but I didn't. Instead, I went in without telling him or having anyone in my corner. As a result, Cassius beat me up so badly in sparring that I walked away with a concussion, a fractured rib, and another blowout fracture, this time in my other eye. I had to pull out of the fight. And Tom was furious.

"So you went and sparred with that animal without telling me? How fuckin' stupid are you? You know it's gonna take even longer to heal and get back in the ring now, right?!"

"Yeah. I just wanted to test myself out and try to show some goodwill so we could get sparring in the future," I said. If you weren't gonna pay for sparring, you needed to barter for it.

Tom took a deep breath and shook his head before continuing.

"Ed, look at your life. You just finished college with a physics degree, and you're making good money from your stuff on social media. You don't need this sport anymore. You can do whatever you want without taking a beating."

A few months earlier, I had taken the Major Field Test in physics. The exam is administered every year to physics students in their final semester of their degree program. The purpose of the test is to measure the effectiveness of the school's program, as well as to see how much you retained and understood. The seventy questions cover every aspect of a typical undergraduate physics program.

I don't know how many of the seventy questions I answered correctly, but I know that I scored better than 65 percent of all graduating physics majors in the country. That year, I was the highest-scoring student in my university's program. This was a major achievement for me, because it was a sign that my plan to improve my mind had worked, just as winning my state boxing title was proof that I had improved my boxing abilities from those of a clumsy novice. Boxing gave me the courage to develop my mind into an asset because it showed me that I could do the same with my body.

A week earlier, I had participated in two affiliate sales that brought in thirty-three thousand dollars. The odds of me ever seeing that type of money in boxing was small, and I'd have to bust my ass ever to touch it.

While I was reflecting on that, Tom continued: "Look, you're my friend. I want to see you get out of this sport without getting hurt. I'll train you if you want me, but as your friend, I'm telling you that you don't need to fight anymore. Think about it."

I spent the next few days considering what he'd said. When I got into boxing, I only envisioned two reasons for quitting: if I got injured to the point where continuing wasn't possible, or if someone I trusted in the sport told me I should get out. Both of those conditions were now staring me in the face. The only question was if I could see myself as something other than a boxer. Would I let myself be dragged into the Fighter's Graveyard or live to transform myself into something new?

While Tom was right about my potential in other areas, this decision was never about the money. A long time ago, I had accepted the possibility of permanent injury (or premature death) from this sport. That said, two incidents from after the sparring injuries kept flashing through my head. In one, I was tutoring one of my students in algebra when my mind started to wander. I couldn't recall the procedure for constructing a polynomial from given roots. Most people do this process the other way around, finding the roots of a given polynomial. This memory lapse alarmed me, because I knew the process, but I couldn't put my brain in reverse. Even more troubling was that I noticed I couldn't read or write more than three to four sentences before I needed to rest. I'd get a headache and need to sleep. With most of my income now coming from my writing abilities, I had to admit that it didn't make sense to put my primary asset—my mental capacity—at risk if I didn't have to.

That risk is acceptable for fighters. We all take it because most of us have no better alternative. However, I now had other options. For people like me who use their minds to support themselves, the risk of losing it outweighs the rewards.

I weighed this fact against the likelihood that I'd ever make as much from boxing as I was making outside of it. I had cleared five figures in the months before the injury and was on pace to do it again. Most boxers will never see a five-figure payday unless they fight for a title or against a big draw on television. And even then, you can only get that type of fight once in your career if you aren't a champ. *Maybe* twice. Former world champion Carl Froch once remarked that approximately 97 percent of fighters either have to get jobs when they stop fighting or work a full-time job while they fight. I'm surprised the figure isn't higher. Every month that year, I made more money than I ever made fighting professionally, even when I fought on TV.

I weighed these things and decided to hang up the gloves. I hesitate to call it retirement, because I could see myself fighting again. I've stayed in great shape to be a sparring partner for guys, but I know how hard it is to find sparring. That's part of what put me in the situation to leave the sport in the first place.

But whatever you call it, in May 2018, my boxing journey ended. Even so, the hard lessons I learned from the hurt business have enriched every area of my life—and they continue to do so.

EPILOGUE

Your Past Doesn't Define Your Future

G ood. You're too smart for boxing."

This is what Charles Martin and Dominic Breazeale both said when they found out that I'd moved on from a thirteen-year boxing career, even though they both had successful careers themselves. Charles had gone on to win the IBF heavyweight title, and Dominic had fought for it twice, losing first to Anthony Joshua and then Deontay Wilder.

Maybe this was true. Then again, how smart was I if I started boxing in the first place?

People often ask me what made me start boxing at the ripe old age of twenty-two. They want to know what would motivate me to put myself in a sixteen-by-sixteen-foot box to fight another human who is trained to inflict significant damage to my person.

Most people run away from fights, or at the very least they try to avoid situations that are guaranteed to cause pain. But not the fighter. In this regard, fighters are built differently than the rest of the population. We are *way* past three standard deviations from the average human when it comes to risk aversion, pain tolerance, and self-regard.

We seek hardship while the masses seek comfort. We confront pain while everyone else pursues pleasure. We walk side by side with uncertainty and fear while most people embrace the safe and sure path. But why do it? Why do we fight?

More specifically, why did *I* do it? Why did I live the life of a fighter for thirteen years?

The Anna Karenina Principle

Every fighter fights for different reasons, but rarely are those reasons born from a state of abundance and fulfillment.

Many people visit the ring for recreation, but those who make it a permanent home do so because they lack something vital, and they feel that they'll find it in the school of hard knocks.

Leo Tolstoy once famously wrote, "All happy families are alike; each unhappy family is unhappy in its own way." This is often referred to as the Anna Karenina principle. The idea is that for a family to be happy regardless of its background or culture, there are certain minimum standards that must be met. Every happy family needs food, shelter, safety, love, etc. However, a deficiency in any one of these areas robs the family of happiness. More generally, happy people have the same things in common, but unhappy people can be unhappy for many reasons, because there are many ways to be unhappy.

The Anna Karenina principle explains why every fighter fights.

All humans have a survival instinct and an aversion to pain. While fighters share this trait with the rest of the population, we believe we'll find what we're missing on the other side of pain. By inflicting pain, we prove that we are worth something, in the most primal and recognizable way. By enduring pain, we prove—in the most defiant and discernible manner—that life is not better than us and cannot beat us down.

I started fighting because I felt like a nobody. I wanted to feel like somebody. I was a twenty-two-year-old college dropout who worked at Starbucks. I hated the feeling of being invisible, insignificant, and overlooked.

I've often said that becoming a fighter to build an identity is like joining the army to learn how to fold your sheets. Sure, you'll get what you came for, but it comes with so much pain, hardship, and restriction that the cost of admission exceeds the value received.

Perhaps there is some truth to this, but this brings me to another reason why I fought.

I realized that I had to deal with the demons holding me back from escaping the familiarity of hell and becoming someone new. Boxing forced me to face parts of me I had never dealt with and tried to drown in alcohol.

I thought I started fighting to become someone special. The real reason was that I never felt like I was good enough to simply be desired in a group. Even now I struggle with this, as I often believe I'm a burden to others—a hard feeling to shake, as it goes all the way back to my early childhood.

But one of the things boxing forced me to do was sell myself. My ability to get people to show up to my fights dictated my ability to get amateur fights in the first place. It wasn't just about training as a professional boxer. My ability to sell myself determined if I got a thousand-dollar check for a fight or barely a hundred dollars—before trainer fees. This meant that I had to get people to support me if I wanted to make it as a fighter—and that meant confronting my fears of inadequacy.

I believe this is why I was pulled to boxing. Boxing served as both a crucible and a distillery, hardening me while removing impurities in my character that kept me from improving. I may have chosen to get in the ring, but I did not get to choose the ways the sport would make me a better person and force me to deal with my weaknesses and fears.

I started fighting to become someone. When I started, I had an immature idea of what that meant, but as I continued with the process and the training, my incomplete ideas were replaced with a richer, more nuanced perspective. When I reflect on my motivations for fighting, I realize that the desire for respect and attention brought me in, but a commitment to what the sport did for me kept me there. I honestly don't know if anything other than boxing would have challenged and transformed me in all the ways it did.

Boxing broke me down, built me up, and made me accountable to the world. It made me a person to be admired and respected. It made me more than I could have ever imagined it would when I first stepped foot in Carrick Community Boxing Academy.

The Path to Forgiveness Is a Journey of Understanding

In 2022, my son was born. Having a new child is one of the most stressful events a person can experience. Yes, we love our children and try to cherish every moment, knowing that one night will be the last time you rock them to sleep, but that doesn't mean it's not a brutal affair. As of this writing, I'm only two years into the journey of parenthood, but it has tested my endurance, decision-making, and patience in ways I've never experienced before—and I'm not a single parent.

This experience has granted me a different perspective and greater sympathy than ever for single parents. I was never bitter about my father's absence. However, throughout my life, I have been heavily critical of my mother for her lifestyle and choices.

Raising a child, even in a two-parent home, is a challenge, but I've been able to meet it with maturity and resources. My wife and I work for ourselves and alternate uninterrupted hours. As a result, we never have to worry about taking parental leave or missing work because our child is sick. We don't worry about finding a babysitter whenever we have an appointment, because the other watches our son. Even something as routine as grocery shopping is a breeze, because someone can stay home rather than navigate the store alone with a fussy toddler. Now that I have a child, I continually think about how difficult it must be to get anything done—even essential tasks—when there's only one parent handling everything.

Single parenting is more than a full-time job. You're free to leave a job at the end of your shift. If you don't like your job, you can get another one. You can even use your time away from work to improve and increase your skill set to get a better-paying, more satisfactory job. However, with single parenting, you're stuck. Also, with each passing year, the job pays you less, as your children demand more resources to survive.

The inability to handle daily affairs is only one facet of a single parent's problem. Without the other parent in the home, there is no reprieve from stress or illness. If a single mother is sick, tired, or worried about something besides her children, she must still be a mom and tend to her kids. She still has to deal with stress from the world and not take it out on them. Of course, this is much easier said than done.

A national survey of six thousand households found single parents to be more likely to use abusive forms of violence toward their children than parents in dual-caretaker households. Lower incomes, the increased stress associated with the sole burden of family responsibilities, and less support to draw on contribute to the increased risk of single parents maltreating their children. With only one parent, every aspect of life is more difficult. The effects of this stress are evident, as the most significant predictor of child abuse is not household income or living in a violent neighborhood. Instead, it's whether the child is primarily cared for by one adult.

Victims of childhood abuse often face harsh futures for many reasons. Too many end up destitute, impoverished, or incarcerated, trying to fill the emotional void left by a lack of guidance, protection, love, and support. Whether through violent acts or substance abuse, these behaviors are often driven by a deep need to belong. But just as often, they're fueled by anger and a profound loss of hope.

When most of your experiences involve disappointment and harm, it's easy to become bitter and sad. If a person spends the first decades of their life in a constant state of fight-or-flight, but with nowhere to run and no way to defend themselves, it's easy to see how one loses faith in humanity and becomes incensed toward it. Studies show that early-life stress alters brain structure and function in ways that precipitate mood disorders like anxiety and depression. These changes in your brain lead to changes in how you perceive the world.

My mother died one year before my son was born. I wish she were still alive so I could tell her that I forgive her for everything, and not only because it would grant me peace of mind. Forgiveness is for me, but the path I took to this place of emotional peace helped me see my parents in a different light. I see my mother as a flawed woman who did the best she could to raise her children despite the physical and sexual abuse she endured growing up and the effects it had on her. Now that I have a son, I recognize that as a single mother, she was doing her best with the few resources and abilities in her possession.

My perspective on my father has also gone through several changes. When I was growing up, we didn't have a relationship.

He'd call once or twice a month, but talking to him always felt like something I was expected to do. It's not that I didn't like talking to my dad. I just did not see him as I imagine you're supposed to see your father. I didn't view him as someone to protect, teach, and guide me. When he visited and took my sister and me around town with him so he could see his friends, I was more excited to have a reprieve from my mom and my neighbor than I was to spend time with him. He never hurt me, but he did not help me either.

In my twenties and most of my thirties, I did not think about him much. I knew that I had a father because I existed, but I couldn't recall anything he taught me, any way he helped me, or any role he played in my life. However, a few years into my sobriety and dealing with the issues that had led to it, I learned about the effect a father's absence has on children. I started to live with a low level of anger that never materialized into outbursts but was always in the background.

This anger briefly intensified the first few months after my son was born. The intensification also brought with it feelings of sadness and confusion. As I held and played with my son, I could not understand how a man could move three hundred miles away, willingly leaving his children behind, and be content to see them for only a few hours each year. There was no one to answer these questions. The only reasoning ever given to me was by my mother, who said, "Your father didn't even want you!" whenever she was angry at us for being excited to see him. Most of my childhood memories of my father didn't disprove her angry outbursts, and hearing that type of thing as a child can have a lasting effect. But one day, I stumbled upon an article that gave me something to help me understand and forgive my father.

According to the Pew Research Center, millennial fathers spend triple the time with their children as did fathers from the Baby Boomer generation, the generation my father belongs to. It was the norm for children who grew up in his generation not to spend much time with their fathers, so, in reality, he saw nothing wrong with leaving us to be cared for by my mother.

Today, the effect of an absent or uninvolved father on children is well-known because of the hundreds of research studies conducted on this issue, but most of that research was performed after 2000. Until recently, a father's role in molding a competent child with the best chance for a successful life was not even considered a problem worth understanding.

While writing this chapter, I had lunch with my uncle. From him, I learned that not only had my dad's father disappeared shortly after he was born, but his mother died when he was four years old. I was unaware of both of these facts. Learning that my father grew up in such tragic and dysfunctional circumstances made a lot of his actions more understandable. His childhood did not justify his absence from mine, but it's easier for me to comprehend if I see it as continuing the behavior modeled for him. From his perspective, even his scant presence in my life was a significant improvement from what he had experienced as a child.

These facts gave me a perspective I could use to extinguish the growing negativity that was beginning to raze my peace of mind and threaten my behavior as a father. My father likely saw nothing wrong with not being an active part of my life. The men from his generation did not emphasize being present in their children's lives, and at that time, most of the population had no idea how impactful a father's presence was. My dad wasn't behaving self-ishly. He was just doing what he knew.

This realization allowed me to forgive him. And by forgiving both him and my mother, I have broken the cycle started by their parents and—who knows?—maybe their parents before them. I won't pass this legacy on to my son: We will start a new pattern based on love, support, and guidance rather than abuse, disap-pointment, and abandonment.

Part of making this happen is forgiving myself as well.

Forgiving Yourself Is More Difficult Than Forgiving Others

Forgiving myself has been the hardest thing I've ever faced. Truth-fully, I'm not even sure I've fully done it, but I try every day. As I write this, I've been sober for ten and a half years. But even after all this time, the guilt lingers. Still, each day is a new chance—one I approach with humility and gratitude for the luck and second chances I've been given.

The main idea I remember when forgiving myself is that the past isn't real. Understanding this concept is crucial to forgiving yourself and others. I'm not implying that what happened in the past is a figment of your imagination, nor am I suggesting that past events don't affect present and future events. More specifically, what I mean is that the past is something that you can't interact with. Just like your imagination takes you to a future location that does not yet exist, your memory takes you to a past that no longer exists. The only difference between memory and imagination is that the yet-to-exist future can be modified by what you do now, but the past cannot be changed.

Consider the implications of this idea as it relates to yourself: You are not the same person who made mistakes in the past. Unless you continue thinking and behaving as you did before, you are a different person. People have difficulty forgiving themselves because they believe they should have known better. They feel guilt because they see who they are now as who they were when they made a mistake. But you are not the same person.

Plenty of physical evidence supports this claim. A surge of hormones floods your body at puberty, changing how you interact with the world. Your brain doesn't finish developing its ability to plan for the future until around thirty. All the cells in your body regenerate every seven to ten years, but there is tremendous variation. Skin cells are replaced every few weeks, while skeletal muscles can take up to fifteen years.

Muhammad Ali once said, "The man who views the world at fifty the same as he did at twenty has wasted thirty years of his life." New experiences and information can instantly change an opinion you held for decades. As you change your perspective, you will inevitably see your old behavior in a new light. You didn't know better then, but now you do.

That said, it's important to take ownership of your past behavior and mistakes. Just because you didn't know better or thought differently does not absolve you of responsibility for your actions. Although I'm making the point of accountability through the lens of self-forgiveness, understanding it will also help with any reservations about forgiving others.

Justice and forgiveness are not substitutes for each other. Justice holds a person accountable for their actions and is carried out as a punitive and preventive measure. Just because we can forgive people doesn't mean we invite them to harm us or others. The purpose of justice is to dissuade people from committing injustices and keep them from harming others in the future.

But sometimes justice feels beyond reach. For example, consider Patrick Crusius, the shooter who murdered twenty-two people in an El Paso mass shooting. The state can only execute him once, and it would do so in a more humane manner than the way he killed his victims. Even the "prison justice" he has likely received won't equal the pain he's caused the families and the fear with which he's infected society. One fewer psycho is on the streets, but that does nothing for the emotional loss and damage the loved ones of the victims suffer. For that, they will have to forgive the emotional debt he caused them. Otherwise, the unchangeable past will always have power over them. Justice prevents him from doing it again, but forgiveness helps the victims release the hold that negative emotions have over them.

When it comes to forgiving yourself, this is the tricky part: How do you enact justice on yourself to ensure that you won't make the same mistake again? And, perhaps more importantly, how do you do this without tightening the grip negative emotions have on your self-worth? This is accomplished by taking accountability, because if you never accept that you made a mistake, there's nothing you can do to prevent it from happening again. There is also nothing you can do to emotionally move past it.

While writing *Sober Letters to My Drunken Self*, my book to help people navigate the emotional turmoil that accompanies sobriety, I felt immense guilt and shame over my previous behavior. I didn't try to ignore or block out those feelings. Rather, I wrote messages that took ownership of my behavior and apologized to every person I had hurt or offended. Some of them responded. Many of them didn't. Their response wasn't necessary. All that mattered was that I took responsibility for my actions.

In talking with other recovering alcoholics, this guilt appears so often that I gave it a name: "Angelus Syndrome," after the character Angel from the TV show *Buffy the Vampire Slayer*, who is cursed to have a soul. Angelus Syndrome is an appropriate name, because you only experience guilt once a fundamental change in you occurs. Angel did not feel remorse until he became, at his core, a new being. Only then could he consider the effects of his past actions with a new conscience.

This guilt is a good thing. It will make you vigilant in the future toward not behaving in a way that requires self-forgiveness. It can also motivate actions to make the world a better place. To make amends for his past actions, Angel hunts other evil supernatural creatures who hurt the world. In a similar fashion, I began to speak at Alcoholics Anonymous meetings and rehab programs and to coach anyone who needed help with sobriety. While these actions make the world a better place, they also help me to forgive myself.

I can't change the past or undo what I've done. The guilt and shame may never fully disappear. But instead of wallowing in them, I've taken steps to forgive myself and use my experiences to help others avoid a similar path. Owning my past helps me live better in the present and build a future where I'll have less to forgive myself for.

Every lesson in this book matters, but I saved this one for last because it's the hardest-earned and most important. I wanted you to know the details of my life—the abuse, the poverty, the alcoholism—so you'd understand that I had plenty to be angry about. But even with all that, I found a way to forgive.

In boxing, victory is clear—determined by whether the referee holds your hand up at the end of the match or someone else's. But in life, victory isn't so simple. True victory in the hurt business of life is forgiving those who've hurt you most. It's one of the few fights where you have complete control over the outcome. It's not a fight you win just once—it's a battle you'll face your entire life. But if you keep fighting the fight, you'll always be a contender.

ACKNOWLEDGMENTS

No one becomes a success on their own. Looking back at how this book came to be, I realize that so many people helped me that it's almost unfair that my name is the only one most people will associate with this project.

Before I name any of those people, I must thank my wife, Anna. She believed in me and my vision when that vision was all I had. She gave birth to our first child right before I started writing this book. While struggling through sleep deprivation, our family relocating to a new home, and running her business, she still gave me time to work on my writing.

Also, a special thank-you to my sister, Jasmine. My memory was shaky regarding specific details, but she helped me fill in the gaps and learn some things that strengthened my story. My uncle Steven gave me some insights into my father's childhood that I didn't have prior to writing this book. Those insights not only helped me write the story but also helped me to make peace with his absence from my childhood.

Next, I appreciate everyone who subscribes to my newsletter, follows me on any social media platform, or shares any of my content. Without you guys, I would be a random writer on the internet. Because you have been kind enough to give me an audience, I got a publishing deal from a major publisher.

Still, having an audience isn't enough. Thank you to Dov Baron for being a friend and introducing me to his agent, Wendy Keller. I took her eight-week intensive workshop on writing a book proposal. I may have never started this journey if it wasn't for her class.

During that class, I talked to every author I knew about what would give me the best chance of securing a book deal. Thank you to Mark Manson, James Clear, Ryan Holiday, Antonio Neves, Jonas Koffler, Chris Wilson, Jon Finkel, Sarah Valentine, and Peter McGraw. A special thank-you to Nat Eliason, Sam Dogen, Jimmy Soni, and Rob Henderson for introducing me to the right people and helping me make the most of those connections.

I must thank Seth Godin for giving me an hour of his time and reminding me that my book will succeed if I can write a story that a few people will talk about passionately. With the social media insights from Alison Rich and Stephanie Bowen, I developed a strategy to grow my LinkedIn presence to connect with a bigger audience. And without the help of Mary Kate Rogers, I might have remained locked out of my Twitter account indefinitely when I fell victim to a hack.

Thanks to Kevin Lincoln for his valuable editorial work and for making my writing the best it could be. Without Kevin, writing this book would have taken at least twice as long and been half as engaging. Along with the heavy editing work provided by Kevin and Noah Schwartzberg, I have to thank Lisa DiVenere and Rachelle Dinishenskaya for reading pieces of the early version and giving me vital feedback that helped me shape the tone of my story.

Speaking of the right people, thank you to my agent, Howard Yoon, for believing in me so much that he signed me in the middle of the biggest merger of his professional career. Howard not only brokered a great book deal but also helped me realize the story I should be telling and package it in a highly appealing fashion.

Thank you to my editor, Noah Schwartzberg. Throughout this project, he's been encouraging me to take my writing to levels I didn't know were possible. He did so while helping me believe more in myself and the power of my story. Thank you to Niki Papadopoulos and Adrian Zackheim for allowing me to get my story to a bigger audience.

Thank you to Dominic Breazeale, Cam F. Awesome, George Fa'avae, Paul Cain, Adam Van Cleave, Mark Yankello, Tom Yankello, Lorenzo Reynolds, and David McWater for answering my questions about the inner workings of AAH, correcting my memories about my time there, clarifying some rules of boxing, and helping me understand how the business of boxing works.

I know an entire team is working hard behind the scenes to ensure this project is beautifully edited and presented. I don't know your names, but your work is the most valuable. Without you guys, I'd be forced to assume so many roles that writing would be an afterthought. If this book is a failure, that's on me. But if it's a success, it's all because you kept a machine going that I know nothing about. Without you, nothing is possible.